W9-AAU-988

A WISH YOU WERE HERE POCKET PORTFOLIO® BOOK

BLUE RIDGE PARKWAY

—ROAD GUIDE—

BY

ROSE HOUK

SIERRA PRESS
MARIPOSA, CA

ACKNOWLEDGMENTS

To a person, National Park Service staff all along the Blue Ridge Parkway were courteous and helpful throughout research on this book. I thank them, and Karen Searle of Eastern National too, for reviews of the manuscript. Jeff Nicholas of Sierra Press has constantly gone the extra mile to make this a readable and visually exciting work, and Nicky Leach performed excellent editing services. Finally, I thank my husband, Michael Collier, who has always traveled with me. —R.H.

The publisher would like to extend his heartfelt thanks to Karen Searle of Eastern National, as well as Mindy DeCesar and Peter Givens, for their time and energy in reviewing Rose's manuscript. And to Rose and her husband, Michael Collier, for their energy, expertise, patience, and fine humor! Every publisher should be so fortunate as to always work with such exceptional people. Bless you all! —J.D.N.

INSIDE FRONT COVER
Dogwood in bloom beside the Parkway, James River Valley. PHOTO ©TERRY DONNELLY

PAGE 2
Sunset over the Blue Ridge Mountains.
PHOTO ©TERRY DONNELLY

TITLE PAGE
The Parkway south of Buck Gap, autumn.
PHOTO ©PAT & CHUCK BLACKLEY

OPPOSITE
The Blue Ridge, autumn near Jumpinoff Rock.
PHOTO ©TIM FITZHARRIS

CONTENTS

OPPOSITE
The Parkway near the Virginia/North Carolina border. PHOTO ©CHARLES GURCHE

BLUE RIDGE PARKWAY: AN INTRODUCTION

I hiked up to Bluff Mountain on a drizzly day in October, through black locust and bittersweet, over slippery wet roots, and past a microcosmic universe of mosses carpeting gray boulders in vivid green. Up on top, I sprawled out on a large flat rock and gazed down on the Blue Ridge Parkway winding through Doughton Park. I imagined the Parkway's visionary planners sitting at this very spot, surveying this same scene, and determining how the road would weave across the ridge here.

The Park-to-Park Highway, as the Parkway was first called, was conceived as an extension of Shenandoah National Park's Skyline Drive, connecting it with the new Great Smoky Mountains National Park in Tennessee. When heated debate ensued in 1933 and 1934 over the Parkway's final route, North Carolina Congressman Robert "Farmer Bob" Doughton, for whom this area is named, evoked the Creator in an impassioned plea to run the road through his state's magnificent mountains. Anyone who viewed this scenery, declared Doughton, "will find that the Omnipotent Architect of the World has carved and chiseled the most outstanding display of nature known to all creation."

As I looked down from my eyrie, I couldn't argue. And I could hardly imagine the Parkway following any path other than the one it follows here across broad meadows and the sawtooth crest of the Blue Ridge Mountains. But for Congressman Doughton and other boosters of the North Carolina route (who were battling Tennessee's bid for the road), some heavy lobbying took place before the decision was made in their favor.

R. Getty Browning, North Carolina Highway Commission engineer, was one of the master promoters of the Parkway. A dedicated outdoorsman, Browning had walked the entire route he favored. He consistently and persuasively stated his belief that the crest of the mountains was the most scenic and least destructive course to take.

Sharing visionary honors was young Stanley Abbott. At age 26 he was appointed the first resident landscape architect of the Blue Ridge Parkway for the National Park Service. From the Westchester, New York, county parks, Abbott arrived in January 1934 to begin his new job—to design the Blue Ridge Parkway. In a truck, with the sketchiest of maps in hand, Abbott traveled, photographed, and described the terrain the Parkway would traverse. He knew that it was to seamlessly connect the Skyline Drive in Shenandoah with the Great Smokies, more than 450 miles away, but believed it had to be more than an ordinary road. It should be a scenic parkway possessing the qualities of variety, simplicity, informality, revelation, and preservation.

TOP: The Parkway near Blowing Rock.
PHOTO ©LAURENCE PARENT
ABOVE: Maple leaf nestled on moss near Bluff Mountain.
PHOTO ©MICHAEL COLLIER

OPPOSITE: The Parkway south of Roanoke, Virginia (aerial view). PHOTO ©MICHAEL COLLIER

TOP: Autumn color at Crabtree Falls.
PHOTO ©PAT & CHUCK BLACKLEY
ABOVE: Fall color at Milepost 417.
PHOTO ©MICHAEL COLLIER

Vistas and scenery, both natural and cultural, were paramount to the design. The Parkway would embrace, rather than deny, the landscape's agricultural life. Fields and fences and old cabins and barns would remain intact or even be moved, and farmers would work as they and their grandfathers had, all so that passing motorists would enjoy an authentic view.

And, said Abbott, every so often there needed to be "a jewel on the string of beads." Thus evolved the planned recreation areas of Peaks of Otter, Rocky Knob, Doughton Park, Julian Price and Moses Cone, Linville Falls, Crabtree Meadows, and Mount Pisgah, each at comfortable intervals of about 60 miles along the drive. In the wake of heavy logging, poor farming, and the road-building itself, the land would also have to be healed.

Abbott's mantra was "marry beauty to utility." This was accomplished through the Planning and Land Use Maps—or "PLUMS"—which meshed the ideas of the landscape architect with the practicalities facing engineers with the federal government's Bureau of Public Roads. Engineering innovations included the spiral transitional curve (a curve of continuously changing radii), used frequently so the Parkway winds like a ribbon through the land. Cross-section cuts were streamlined rather than abrupt. Many other subtle details consciously and skillfully "mold the Parkway to the mountains." Every bridge, tunnel, culvert, fence, sign, and building, even the omission of striping on the shoulders of the road, assure that the Parkway blends harmoniously with the natural environment.

From my perch atop Bluff Mountain, I began to appreciate the genius of the Parkway's planners. The more time I spend here, the more I realize that the Blue Ridge Parkway is much more than a road. It's a scrapbook, a photo album, a place to be experienced with all my senses. I taste the tart sweetness of an apple from a wizened old tree at Big Spy Mountain. I hear water splashing over the big overshot wheel at Mabry Mill. I see an old log cabin and listen to two women talking softly on the porch as they stitch a friendship quilt. I remember a country store, whose proprietor shares a lifetime of tales with anyone who will stay and listen. I gasp at Catawba rhododendrons dressing up the roadside in gaudy pink in May, and marvel at the perfect, exquisite beauty of Crabtree Falls. I grin at the sight of a chubby groundhog sitting upright along the roadside. I savor the warmth of the fireplace inside the visitor station high up on Waterrock Knob, on a cold, fogbound spring day. I sense the spirits of the Cherokee who roamed these mountains, and wonder at the whimsy of the folk artist who carved two bluebirds scolding each other over a pine cone.

Always I look around the next curve, anticipating another inspiring vista, a fabulous waterfall, the peaceful, unhurried rambling that defines a trip on the Blue Ridge Parkway.

Boulders at sunset, Peaks of Otter. PHOTO ©CHARLES GURCHE

THE APPALACHIAN MOUNTAINS

From the platform of the Blue Ridge Parkway, standing on the oldest mountains in the country, millions of people each year gaze at the awesome sights of cloud-ruffed crests, tumbling streams, and rain-drenched forests.

Lean closer and touch the rock. It is ancient beyond anything we can fathom in our short life span. Much of the rock of the Appalachian Mountains is so old that it's been changed beyond recognition from its origins, so old that no life forms have been preserved, so old that entire continents and oceans have come and gone since it formed.

The oldest rocks in the Appalachians are between one and two billion years in age—schists, gneisses, and granites—the roots of a mountain range produced by a slow, grinding collision of continents. Those mountains were worn down, followed by pulses of more mountain-building. The last one took place about 250 million to 300 million years ago, when Ancestral Africa and North America slammed head-on in the "Grand Collision."

The massive crumpling and folding of the land created a towering range, perhaps 3,000 to 4,000 feet higher than today's Appalachians. Ice, water, and wind have nipped and tucked the highlands into a range of forested ridges and valleys and coves.

The modern Appalachians mark the horizon for 1,600 miles from Newfoundland to central Alabama. They achieve greatest expression in the central and southern reaches as the misty Blue Ridge Mountains, where they branch into a complex and rugged system of ranges. North Carolina's Mount Mitchell, at 6,684 feet elevation, stands as the highest peak in the eastern United States; another 50 or so summits also exceed 6,000 feet.

PAGE 12/13: Looking Glass Rock. PHOTO ©MICHAEL COLLIER

APPALACHIAN MOUNTAIN CULTURE

More than anything, the Blue Ridge Mountains are the mountains of home. They are a place where a weathered-gray log cabin poses in quiet simplicity, sheltered by the spreading arms of a venerable oak tree. Where a rocking chair on a cool, shaded porch beckons a person to sit and stitch a quilt. Where a cantilevered barn, golden hay spilling from the loft, speaks of a farmer husbanding his fields and animals. And where a banjo or berry basket kindle memories of a life of music and bounty.

Indians called these mountains home for thousands of years before whites arrived. They stalked bison, harvested plants, cultivated corn, and mined mica and soapstone. The most recent were the better-known Cherokee of North Carolina and the lesser-known Monacan, Saponi, and Tutelo people in Virginia. Each group claimed territory, each had stories of how they and the mountains came to be. That all unraveled when Europeans pushed into the mountain frontier from the lowlands, lured by good land and, in some cases, refuge from persecution. Although the newcomers eventually drove the Indians into ever tighter corners, native people passed along a vast store of experiences and knowledge about living in these highlands.

By the 1750s, Germans were traveling south from Pennsylvania into the Shenandoah Valley, then up into the Blue Ridge after the best valley land was taken. There were English and Celts, too, but mainly the Scots–Irish pressed in the greatest numbers. Many stayed and melded their own traditions with adaptations to the new place—cobbling together a unique Appalachian Mountain culture.

Upon arrival, a settler's first order of business was to carve a small clearing out of the dense forest. Trees were cut down, girdled, or burned. In those days the woods were filled with American chestnut trees, whose wood was preferred for a log cabin. With meager metal tools—usually only an ax, an adze, and a froe—a pioneer hewed the chestnut logs straight and true, notched the ends, then laid them up one-story high, sometimes with a sleeping loft. He chinked the spaces between with mud, stones, and wood, and roofed the cabin with white oak "shake" shingles. A pure source of water—a "bold" spring—was a prerequisite for a desirable home.

With a roof over their heads, a family then turned attention to food. The forest and streams teemed with bear, deer, 'possums, groundhogs, trout, and turtles. Plants like pokeweed, ramps, mints, mushrooms, berries, and nuts were abundant and edible. In the garden grew neat rows of potatoes, turnips, beans, cabbage, and sometimes an orchard of apple, peach, and plum trees. Most families raised a few chickens for eggs and meat; a cow for milk, cream, and butter;

TOP: Farmland near Whetstone Ridge. PHOTO ©PAT & CHUCK BLACKLEY
ABOVE: Detail of barn construction, Mountain Farm display at Humpback Rocks. PHOTO ©MICHAEL COLLIER

OPPOSITE: The William Ramsey Cabin at Mountain Farm, Humpback Rocks. PHOTO ©PAT & CHUCK BLACKLEY

TOP: Tobacco drying at the Johnson Farm, Peaks of Otter.
PHOTO ©MICHAEL COLLIER
ABOVE: Rocky Knob Cabin.
PHOTO ©MICHAEL COLLIER

and a few razorback hogs for ham, bacon, and lard. The food was eaten either fresh from the field or dried, smoked, salted, pickled, or canned.

Sugar was hard to come by, so honey and molasses satisfied a sweet tooth. After catching a swarm of honeybees, a beekeeper housed them in the hollow stump of a black gum—thus the "beegum." Green liquid from crushed sorghum cane was simmered and skimmed all day, then bottled as liquid gold.

Corn was turned into liquid form too, commonly called moonshine. Another fine Scots-Irish tradition—distilling one's own liquor—fit well with the mountain philosophy of self-suffiency. Tucked away down by a stream in a discreet thicket of rhododendron, a still usually consisted of a wood-stoked furnace and a copper barrel in which a fermented mixture of ground corn, malt, rye, water, and sometimes sugar, was boiled. The steam that was produced went through a copper pipe and down a spiraled tube, the "worm," cooling and condensing into a liquid. Moonshine was filtered through hickory coals, then funneled into a jug, barrel, or Mason jar. For a time it was legal to make and sell liquor—and many people did so as a source of income. Then the federal government started taxing and requiring a license. In 1919 Prohibition made the making and selling of alcoholic beverages illegal in the country, and enforcement of the law sometimes carried political overtones. Said mountain fiddle player Tommy Jarrell, "The Republicans came in and cut all the Democrats' stills, and left the Republicans' stand."

Nearly everything pioneers needed came from the ground and their own hands. But the most utilitarian items were beautifully crafted—baskets woven of oak, hickory, and river cane; quilts from brightly colored flour sacks; coverlets of handspun yarn dyed an earthy brown with walnut hulls; a ladderback chair turned by hand and assembled without a nail or screw. Even a child's toys—cornhusk dolls and geehaw whimmy diddles—were made from what was free and plentiful.

Neighbors were often few and far between, but mountain folk weren't as isolated as some stereotypes imply. They traded goods with lowland communities, and tourists were journeying up to mountain resorts early in the 19th century. On mill day people gathered and caught up on news and gossip while they waited their turn to have their corn ground into meal. When someone needed help with a big job like raising a barn or shucking corn, everyone pitched in.

Mountain people, like most rural Americans of the period, believed the devil was a powerful force to be reckoned with, and o religion guided their daily lives. Impeccable country churches—mostly Methodist, Baptist, and Presbyterian—stood elegantly in whitewashed siding and shuttered windows. Congregations filled the pews on Sunday mornings, which sometimes stretched into all-day singing and "dinner on the grounds." In the absence of a full-time preacher, people waited for the circuit-rider to make his rounds on horseback to perform baptisms and weddings. And when a person was called to his Maker, he or she would be buried in the family cemetery beside the church and the grave lovingly tended.

Music wafted up out of the mountains like the filmy mist that combs the hills and hollows. Nearly anywhere, anytime, someone would pick up a banjo, fiddle, guitar, mandolin, or dulcimer and start to play. At a camp meeting, on a front porch, or in a grove of trees, they played and sang the old Scottish or Irish ballads, hymns, and gospels about family, home, love, and death. When times were bad, said one man, they "sang their misery out." And once the music got going, it was impossible to sit still. Anywhere but church, people were soon on their feet clogging and flatfooting.

The humor and poetry of mountain people still shines in their fine-honed storytelling—tales of "haints" and heroes, bears and battles—passed down by word of mouth from father to son and mother to daughter. The Hicks family, from near Boone, North Carolina, are famed storytellers. Ray Hicks would wrap all seven feet of his lanky frame into a chair and spin out a yarn. Often it was a "Jack tale," about a humble man or boy who outwits powerful people or forces.

All these things—shelter, food, crafts, religion, music, and stories—add up to a way of life that still clings to the Blue Ridge Mountains, like the greenbrier vining up the trunk of a hickory tree. They all add up to that place called home.

TOP: Autumn sunset at Mabry Mill.
PHOTO ©TOM ALGIRE
ABOVE: Moonshine still on display at Mabry Mill.
PHOTO ©MICHAEL COLLIER

VISITING THE BLUE RIDGE PARKWAY

Once you start down the Blue Ridge Parkway, savoring the leisurely pace it affords, you won't want to leave. Should you be forced to leave for necessary services, you'll eagerly return to the sanity and sanctity of this pleasure road.

The Parkway is a completely noncommercial, two-lane paved road, 469 miles in length, through Virginia and North Carolina. Simple concrete posts mark each mile. Maximum driving speed is 45 miles an hour, and you could drive straight through in only 11 hours. But who would want to? The whole point of the Parkway is to drive a while, stop a while, explore a while. And there are plentiful opportunities to do so.

Frequent waysides and pulloffs frame stunning views of thick forest and ranks of silhouetted mountains as far as the eye can see. Plaques at the overlooks relate the region's unique history and interesting natural features—such as how to distinguish the four different kinds of hickory trees that grow here. Larger developed areas, with campgrounds, lodges, and places to eat, invite longer stays.

Fourteen National Park Service visitor centers let you deepen your interests with exhibits, book sales, maps, and other items. Ranger-led walks and talks around the campfire, primarily offered in summer, lend a personal touch, as do living history demonstrations at places like Humpback Rocks and Mabry Mill. Visitor centers are usually open May through October—depending on conditions—except for the Museum of North Carolina Minerals (MP 331) and the Folk Art Center (MP 382), which are open year-round.

The Parkway has nine campgrounds, with tent and recreational vehicle sites. Most are first-come, first-serve. Camping is also available in surrounding national forests, state parks, and commercial enterprises. Parkway campgrounds do not have utility hookups, showers, or laundry facilities. Concession-run accommodations include four lodges and rustic cabins, and six restaurants and coffee shops. Thirteen picnic areas have some facilities, and many waysides have picnic tables as well. Fires are permitted only in campgrounds and picnic areas.

At least 100 hiking trails can be reached from the Parkway, from short, welcome leg-stretchers to longer circuit and loop hikes. The Appalachian Trail, which runs from Maine to Georgia, is accessible at points along the first 100

TOP: Wildcat Rocks, Doughton Park. PHOTO ©TIM FITZHARRIS
MIDDLE: Flame azaleas. PHOTO ©TOM ALGIRE
BOTTOM: Fly amanita mushrooms. PHOTO ©ADAM JONES

OPPOSITE: Autumn along the Parkway, Milepost 453. PHOTO ©MICHAEL COLLIER

PAGE 20/21: Sunset near the highest point on the Parkway in Virginia. PHOTO ©CARR CLIFTON

ABOVE: Morning fog at Flat Top Manor, Moses H. Cone Memorial Park. PHOTO ©LAURENCE PARENT
TOP RIGHT: Lichen-encrusted rock and forest in fog. PHOTO ©CARR CLIFTON
BOTTOM RIGHT: Pinnacle Ridge tunnel. PHOTO ©MICHAEL COLLIER

miles of the Parkway in Virginia. Other activities include road bicycling, photography, fishing, hang gliding, and non-motorized boating on lakes (canoes and rowboats can be rented at Price Lake). Swimming is not allowed in the park, nor is hunting.

Most facilities and services are open and available May through October. State and federal roads provide access to full services in neighboring towns. Few pay phones are available anywhere along the Parkway. The Parkway passes through 26 tunnels—lowest clearance is 10 feet, 6 inches.

With elevations ranging from about 650 feet to more than 6,000 feet, weather can vary dramatically in a single day. Foggy conditions are common, and ice and snow in winter can close sections of the Parkway. Traffic can be heavy on certain weekends, and motorists are advised to use caution pulling in and out of overlooks. Always be aware of wildlife crossing the road.

BUILDING THE BLUE RIDGE PARKWAY

The idea of a "pleasure road along the summit of the Blue Ridge" dates back at least to 1906, when North Carolina geologist Joseph Hyde Pratt observed that the grand scenery of these mountains would furnish a ride "never to be forgotten." Construction of the road did begin in those early years, but World War I scuttled Pratt's dream.

Heavy promotion by tourism and business interests rekindled the idea in the early 1930s, when the despondency of the Great Depression lent more impetus to the project. Men in the Appalachian Mountains were unemployed, and their wives and children were hungry. Road construction jobs, even at $55 a week, could be their ticket out of grim poverty.

President Franklin Delano Roosevelt, Interior Secretary Harold Ickes, Virginia Senator Harry Byrd, various congressmen, and state leaders all endorsed the prospect of putting 10,000 people to work and luring visitors to the region.

No time was wasted. The National Industrial Recovery Act of 1933 gave birth to the Public Works Administration, and more important it funded projects such as the Blue Ridge Parkway. After the route was settled in late 1934, surveyors, engineers, and landscape architects swarmed into the mountains to lay out the road. The state and federal governments had to negotiate sometimes contentious rights-of-way and easements with many private land owners, who were soon calling the road "the Scenic." Even while that was happening, the first construction contract for the Parkway was let in August 1935, and the first shovelful of dirt was turned a month later at the Virginia-North Carolina border near Cumberland Knob.

Blasting, drilling, clearing, grading, cutting, filling, and planting were accomplished with steam shovels, trucks, road-graders, and sheer manual labor. Private contractors and men in the Civilian Conservation Corps and other federal projects did the bulk of the work. The skilled masonry of the stone walls, culverts, and curbs remains a work of art.

The Parkway was completed in unconnected sections. After a brief hiatus during World War II, road-building began again, and by the mid 1960s all but 7 1/2 miles around Grandfather Mountain were done. With completion of the Linn Cove Viaduct, that portion was finished too.

In 1987, 52 years after construction began, the "pleasure road" along the crest of the beautiful Blue Ridge Mountains finally was complete: 469 miles, 26 tunnels, nearly 170 bridges, 264 scenic pullouts, and 9 major recreational areas, at a cost of $124 million.

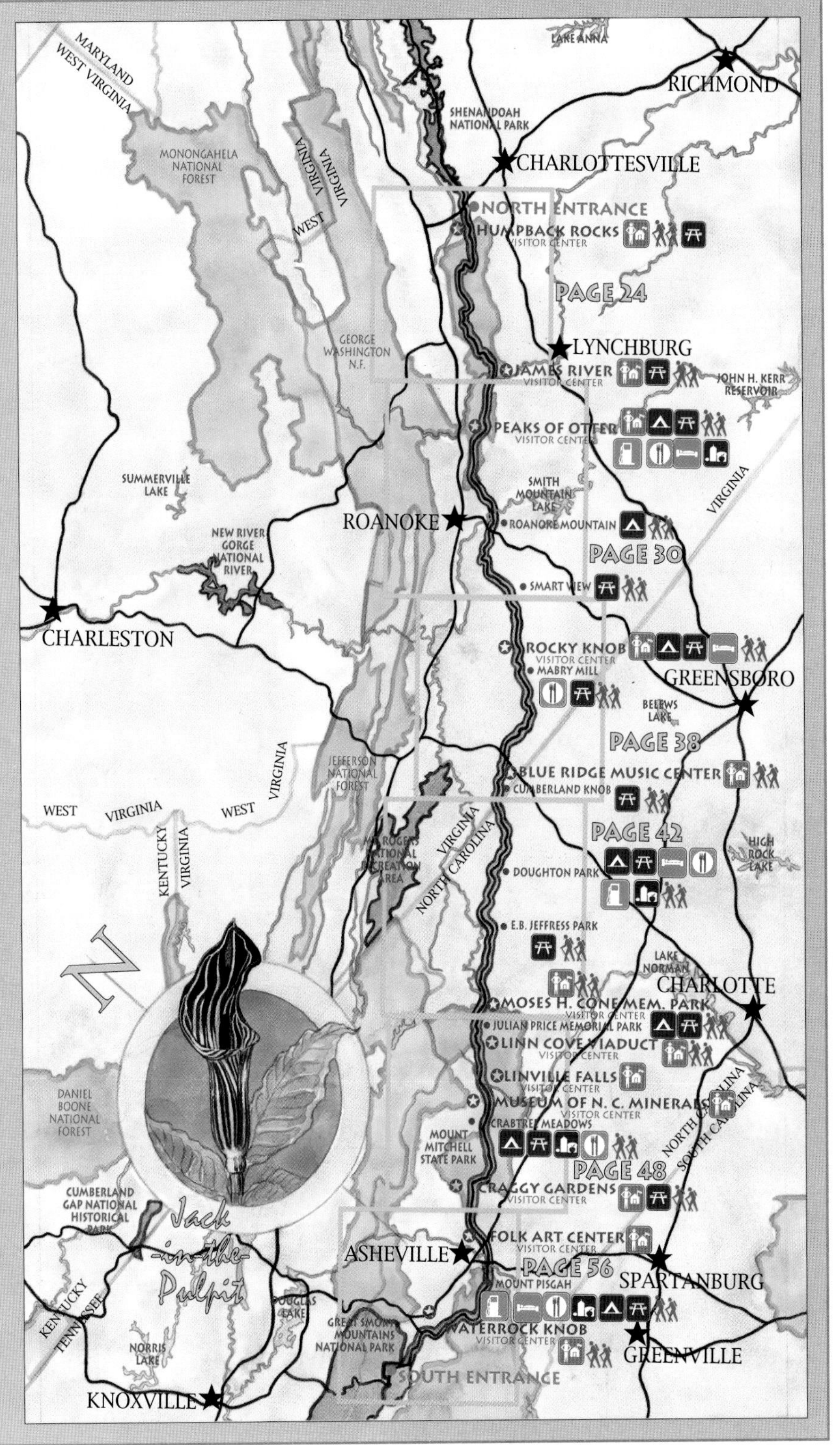

ILLUSTRATION BY DARLECE CLEVELAND

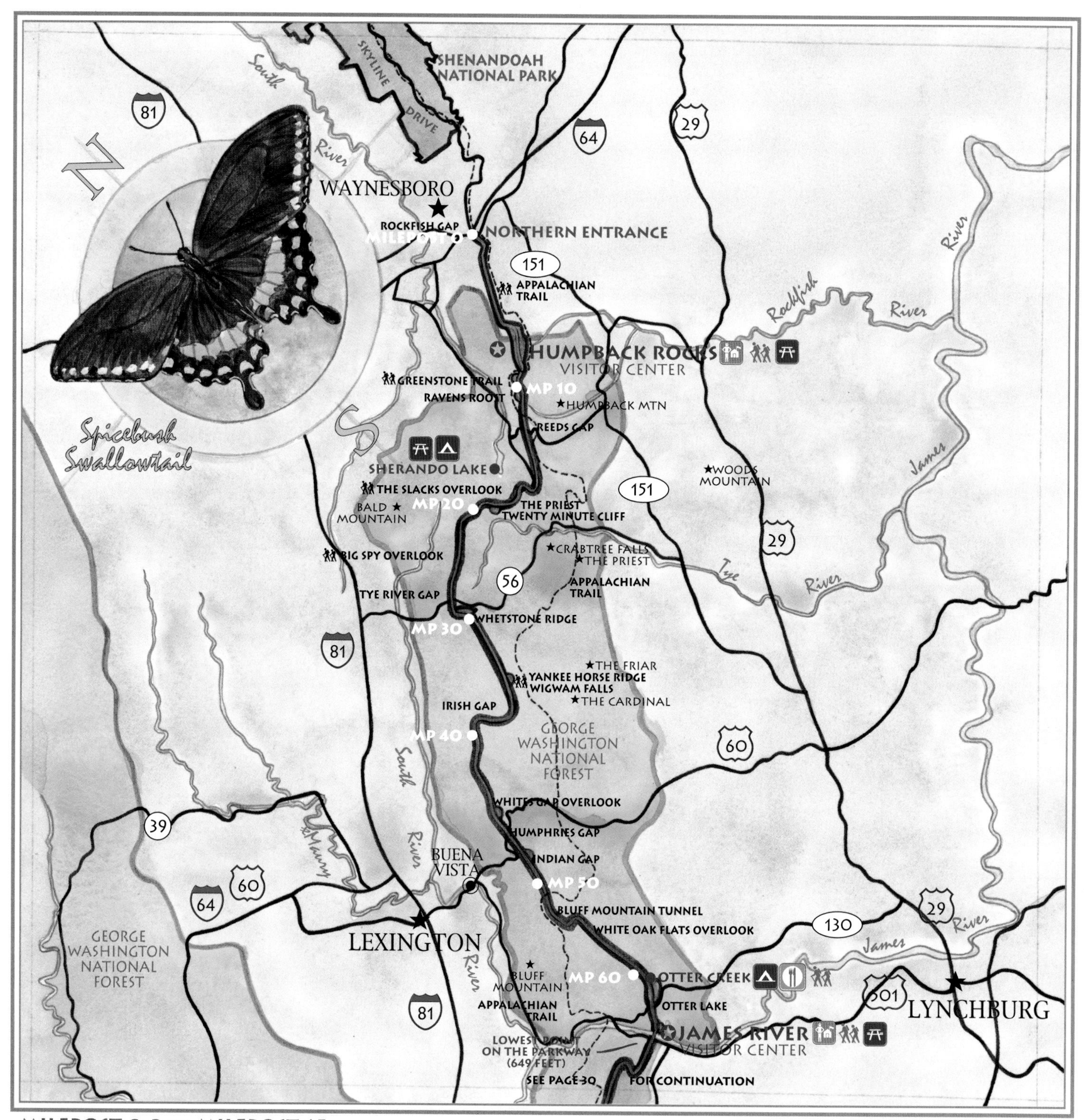

MILEPOST 0.0 TO **MILEPOST 65**

ILLUSTRATION BY DARLECE CLEVELAND

NORTH ENTRANCE TO JAMES RIVER

MILEPOST 0. North Entrance, Rockfish Gap. In the early 1850s, a woman riding in a carriage at Rockfish Gap wrote ecstatically that "We were, both literally and figuratively, *up in the clouds*. . . .Oh, if I could always behold such scenes, I think I could be better and purer—less selfish and worldly-minded."

This gap links the Rockfish Valley on the east and Shenandoah Valley to the west. The Crozet Tunnel was built 510 feet beneath the gap in 1858; Stonewall Jackson took troops through here during the Civil War. Relief map in chamber of commerce information center; I-64 and US 250 cross here.

5.8. Humpback Rocks. Small visitor center with excellent exhibits on the region's early residents, their schools, churches, music, and ties to the outside world—mainly via the old Howardsville Turnpike, a major route for moving goods in the 19th century.

A self-guiding trail leads out to the Mountain Farm, a typical pioneer homestead consisting of five buildings placed on what was originally the William Carter farm. The 1890s log cabin is permeated with the scent of old wood, smoke, and apples. It belonged to William Ramsey who lived about 45 miles away. Friendly volunteers in period clothing relate the story of the farm, while the resident rooster, Mr. Dumpling, crows his heart out.

The Humpback Rocks themselves are a landmark, accessible by a steep, one-mile trail leading from the Humpback Gap Parking Area across the road from the farm.

6.0. Appalachian Trail. The "AT," marked with white blazes along its 2,100-mile length from Maine to Georgia, passes through this overlook. Around mile 98 on the Parkway, the AT veers west, headed for the Great Smokies. A trail climbs steeply for a mile up to Humpback Rocks.

8.8. Greenstone Trail. A 0.2-mile walk amid basalt outcrops. The rock is Catoctin Greenstone, volcanic in origin, then slightly metamorphosed and uplifted as part of the Appalachian Mountains. Abundant lichens and mosses emboss the boulders, and minerals impart the greenish hue. Greenstone is the most common rock type at the north end of the Parkway.

10.7. Ravens Roost. Inky black ravens perch on a rock ledge here. Watch for these aerobatic birds, along with hang gliders and rock climbers.

13.5. Reeds Gap. VA 664 Crossover, AT Crossing

16.0. Sherando Lake. George Washington National Forest recreation area, 4.5 miles west of the Parkway on VA 814, camping, swimming, boating, fishing

17.6. The Priest. The Priest is one of several peaks—along with The Friar, Cardinal, and Little

TOP: Sunset, Humpback Rocks. PHOTO ©CHARLES GURCHE
MIDDLE: Tobacco curing at Mountain Farm. PHOTO ©JEFF D. NICHOLAS
BOTTOM: Shenandoah Valley seen from Ravens Roost. PHOTO ©PAT & CHUCK BLACKLEY

TOP: Otter Creek. PHOTO ©MICHAEL COLLIER
BOTTOM: Wigwam Falls.
PHOTO ©PAT & CHUCK BLACKLEY

Priest—in this range. In truth, the mountain's name is for the de Priest family.

20.0. The Slacks Overlook. White Rock Falls Trail departs north of this parking area, 2.6 miles down to White Rock Falls and back, or 4.5 miles back to Sherando Campground. Traveling south along this portion of the Parkway, the narrow ridge breaks up into more complex topography.

26.3. Big Spy Overlook. Old apple trees at this overlook still bear fruit in the fall. A short loop trail leads up to a bench and an expansive view, indicating why this was a good lookout point for troops during the Civil War.

27.0. Tye River Gap. VA 56 Crossover.

34.4. Yankee Horse Ridge Parking Area. A 200-foot section of the South River Lumber Company's narrow-gauge rail and trestle are reconstructed here. The Irish Creek Railway was built in 1919-1920 to transport millions of board feet of virgin timber out of the mountains. The Yankee Horse Trail is an easy 0.2-mile walk to a footbridge at the foot of lovely Wigwam Falls.

45.6. Humphries Gap. US 60 Crossover.

53.1. Bluff Mountain Tunnel. The first of 26 tunnels along the Parkway; all are in North Carolina except this one.

55.2. White Oak Flats Overlook. A brief streamside walk is possible here.

60.8. Otter Creek. The campground offers pleasant sites along Otter Creek, and the coffee shop serves a superb homemade berry cobbler. At the campground registration station, a checker-board mounted on a stump, with two facing chairs, invites contenders to sit and play a game. From the campground, the Otter Creek Trail leads eventually (3.5 miles) to the James River Visitor Center. You'll cross and recross the creek over stepping stones.

61.4. VA 130 Crossover.

63.1. Otter Lake. A couple of parking places along the lake and at the dam allow access to Otter Lake Loop Trail, described as an "intensely scenic" walk of about a mile.

63.2. Lowest point on Parkway, 649 feet above sea level.

63.6. James River. See Page 30.

FARM LIFE AT HUMPBACK ROCKS

The Ramsey family's one-room cabin with loft is a classic Blue Ridge Mountain home. With ax, maul, froe, and adze, a pioneer hewed chestnut logs for the cabin walls and white pine planks for the floor. Every type of wood had a particular quality suited to a particular use—water-resistant chestnut for buildings, oak or pine for "shakes"or shingles, black locust for pegs, yellow poplar or pine for floors. The cabin's large stone fireplace took up one wall, for heating and cooking. The front porch was the setting for many pleasant hours spent strumming a dulcimer or stitching a quilt.

Of great concern to all pioneer settlers were their animals. The Ramsey cabin's peephole, or "predator window," let someone peer out and spot marauding animals like bears or mountain lions headed for the cows or chickens. As additional protection, the chicken house was weasel-proofed with wood chinking.

Families needed all the food they could grow and preserve, and out in the garden were rows of corn, beans, potatoes, cabbage, tobacco, and broom corn. Blue Ridge farmers planted by the "signs" and the phases of the moon, and worried about killing frosts, voracious crows, and times of drought.

The meathouse/root cellar was set into the hillside, meathouse on the upper level and rock-walled root cellar on the lower. Potatoes, turnips, and other crops were stored inside for the winter, along with a few barrels of pickled beans or corn. Down the path stands the barn, 16 feet by 16 feet, shingled with split white oak, serving several functions as stable, corn crib, and cowshed. It was sited to avoid harsh north winds, and the door let in the warm morning sun. Razorback hogs were allowed to run loose in the woods, but they knew what was happening when they were brought into the stone-encircled pig pen at slaughter time.

Down at the springhouse, water was channeled into a stone trough, keeping it pure for drinking and providing a cool refrigerator for milk, butter, and eggs. Placed conveniently nearby were the iron kettle for washing clothes, and a "beetling" block where clothes were beaten, or "beetled,"with a paddle on washday. Wood ashes were filtered in a wooden trough to make lye for soap. The gate at the end of the walk pivots on one post, cleverly counterbalanced with fieldstones inside a hollow log—it was a style common when hardware and metal tools were hard to come by.

Barn at the Mountain Farm exhibit, Humpback Rocks. PHOTO ©CHARLES GURCHE

PAGE 28/29: Autumn color seen from Bluff Mountain Overlook. PHOTO ©TIM FITZHARRIS

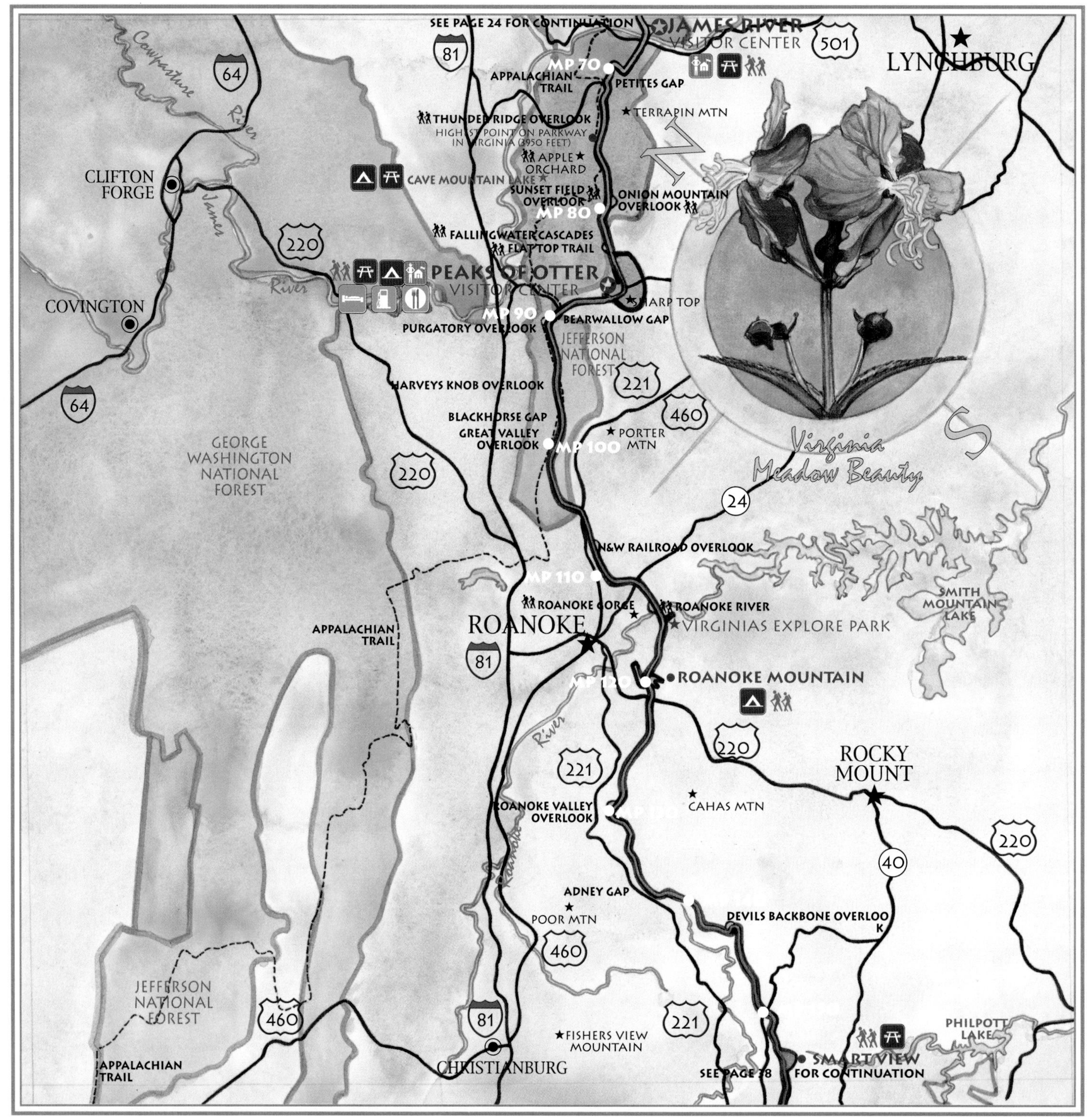

MILEPOST 63 TO MILEPOST 155

ILLUSTRATION BY DARLECE CLEVELAND

JAMES RIVER TO SMART VIEW

63.6. James River. Parkway visitor center stands at the James River Water Gap, a place where water eroded rocks. The center has an information desk, sales area, and nice picnic spot outside beside the river. You can learn about local tree species along the half-mile, self-guided Trail of Trees.

The James River Canal Trail displays another interesting piece of Blue Ridge history. The walk leads over the wide James River under the Parkway bridge, then goes down to the James River & Kanawha Canal. The idea, an old one, was to connect the James with the New River into the Ohio River drainage. From about 1850 to 1880, tow barges and packet boats regularly carried wheat, tobacco, and pig iron upstream from coastal areas and the Piedmont. But getting through the barrier of the mountains was a costly, difficult task that was never accomplished.

The Battery Creek Lock was used to lift or lower boats safely up from the river or down to it. Along the canal towpath, a man with stock animals pulled the boats along. This was one of 90 such locks in the 206 miles of canal eventually built between Richmond and Buchanan.

63.9. US 501 Crossover.

74.7. Thunder Ridge Overlook. Ten-minute walk to look out on Arnold Valley, named for an 18th-century settler. Access to AT and Hunting Creek Trail.

76.5. Apple Orchard Parking Area. The Parkway gains nearly 3,000 feet elevation from the James River to Apple Orchard. Apples weren't grown here; instead, the name is for the wind-pruned northern red oaks known locally as "orchards." In 0.2 mile, travelers reach the highest point on the Parkway in Virginia—3,950 feet.

78.4. Sunset Field Overlook. Gaze out on the Great Valley of Virginia and walk the 1.4-mile trail, down 1,000 feet to 150-foot Apple Orchard Falls. It's another 1.4 miles back out. If it's late in the day, the reward may be a gorgeous sunset. Connection with the AT on Parker's Gap Road (Forest Service Road 812).

83.1. Fallingwater Cascades Parking Area. A 1.6-mile loop trail goes to Fallingwater Cascades, with stone steps down to the creek, a footbridge, and views of the waterfall.

83.5. Flat Top Trail. This National Recreation Trail continues 4.4 miles to Peaks of Otter picnic area, through a profuse growth of wildflowers at certain times of the year.

85.5-86.0. Peaks of Otter/Johnson Farm. A big center of activity on the Parkway, Peaks of Otter includes a lodge, campground, picnic area, and visitor center. The lodge and dining room look out on tranquil Abbott Lake, honoring Parkway landscape architect Stanley Abbott. The

TOP: Sharp Top Mountain, Peaks of Otter. PHOTO ©CHARLES GURCHE
BOTTOM: Roanoke River Gorge, early morning. PHOTO ©JEFF D. NICHOLAS

TOP: Footbridge and rhododendrons in fog, Fallingwater Cascades Trail. PHOTO ©PAT & CHUCK BLACKLEY
BOTTOM: Polly Wood's "Ordinary", Peaks of Otter. PHOTO ©MICHAEL COLLIER

aptly named Sharp Top Mountain rises behind the lake. It, along with Flat Top and Harkening Hill, make up the Peaks of Otter. There probably weren't any river otters, but a rare amphibian, the Peaks of Otter salamander, does live here. The name may have derived from a Cherokee word for high places, for the headwaters of the Otter River, or from the area's resemblance to the homeland of Scottish settlers.

From the 1830s to the 1850s, travelers stabled their horses and rested and dined at Polly Wood's Ordinary. Mary "Polly" Wood ran her humble home as an inn, attending to people's "ordinary" needs. Later, guests escaped the sultry lowlands to relax at the more spacious Hotel Mons, where advertisements promised "the nights are restful and slumber inviting." The building was taken down in the early 1940s.

A 0.7-mile trail leads from near the visitor center to the Johnson Farm. It started as the Peaks of Otter community in 1766, with settler Thomas Wood, then was owned by John and Mary Johnson. Three generations of the Johnson and Bryant families lived here from 1852 to 1941. The whitewashed clapboard house, surrounded by a neat picket fence, has been restored to the 1920s appearance when the last Johnson descendant lived here. The farm includes fruit trees, springhouse, smokehouse, barn, beegum, and a garden with a pair of whimsical scarecrows. Children could not have resisted climbing into the gnarled branches of the grandmother apple tree. Hanks of tobacco cure on the side of a building, and the shaded porch would have been a haven when work was done on a hot summer day.

Along with the Johnson Farm Trail, other trails lead to Elk Run, Harkening Hill, and Sharp Top. For those who would rather ride, a bus goes up from the visitor center to Sharp Top on a regular schedule during season. There is a charge.

91.0. Bearwallow Gap. VA 43 Crossover; the AT crosses under the Parkway.

95.3. Harveys Knob Overlook. A premier hawk-watching location in the fall. Though the grand migration of broad-wing hawks is mostly done by the end of September, a number of other species still fly over in October and into November. Roanoke-area birders set up lawn chairs here and keep daily tallies—on one spectacular day in October they counted 15 osprey, 1 bald eagle, 6 northern harriers, 22 sharp-shinned hawks, 4 Cooper's hawks, 15 broad-wings, 2 redtails, 1 kestrel, 2 merlins, 2 peregrine falcons, and untold numbers of turkey vultures!

106.0. US 460 Crossover. To Roanoke, Virginia, largest city along the Parkway. Suburbs and other buildings press close in to the road's right-of-way.

106.9. N&W Railroad Overlook. The Norfolk & Western Railroad carried coal from West Virginia. During Roanoke's annual Railway Festival, steam locomotives chug onto the tracks.

112.2. VA 24 Crossover.

114.9. Roanoke River Parking Area. After crossing the Roanoke River bridge, a 0.4-mile, self-guiding trail drops into the gorge and down to the tree-lined river. Geologists consider the Roanoke River the dividing line between the central and southern Appalachian Mountains.

115.0. Virginia's Explore Park. 1.5 miles off Parkway, this private park features visitor center, reconstructed historic buildings, living history talks, trails, and special events. Admission fee.

120.3-120.4. Roanoke Mountain Loop Road. A 4-mile drive near top of Roanoke Mountain, with views of the city and the valley and a short trail to the mountain summit. Mill Mountain Spur Road leads to Roanoke Mountain Campground, Mill Mountain park and zoo, and additional trails. At the campground, wooden platforms and a small stage host scheduled Sunday evening gatherings of mountain music and clogging (check the Parkway's website for scheduled events).

121.4. US 220 Crossover.

136.0. Adney Gap. Thomas Adney had a hemp mill here in the late 1700s. For the next 200 miles south, the Parkway follows the edge of the Blue Ridge Plateau, past rolling farmlands with bales of hay and happy cows. The crest of the Blue Ridge marks the eastern continental divide—streams flowing east enter the Atlantic Ocean, while those flowing west enter the Gulf of Mexico.

154.5. Smart View Parking Area. See Page 38.

TOP: Sharp Top Mountain and Abbott Lake at sunrise, Peaks of Otter. PHOTO ©PAT & CHUCK BLACKLEY
BOTTOM: The James River. PHOTO ©JEFF D. NICHOLAS

FOODS OF THE BLUE RIDGE

Traditional mountain foods may not be the first things that come to mind with the Blue Ridge Parkway. But visitors will find plenty of chances to partake of regional specialties such as fresh-ground cornmeal, country ham, and apple butter. The miller at Mabry Mill (MP 176) insists that cornmeal stone ground "to the consistency of sand" makes the best breads.

The Mabry Mill restaurant is famous for corn cakes, served hot and steaming for breakfast. Ham, the only meat worthy of the name to most mountain folk, is also on the menu. You have two choices—city ham and country ham. The waitress will explain the difference (though it's transparently clear which is superior). City ham, she drawls softly, is what you buy in the grocery store wrapped in brown plastic. "Country ham is really special. It's salty, so you'll want to have a glass of water with it. But water's good for you."

In October at the mill, apple butter is made the old-fashioned way, outdoors over an open fire in a big copper kettle, stirred with a long-handled wooden paddle, preferably of white poplar. Here's the recipe: Peel, core, and slice four or five bushels of apples—Rome Beauties, Jonathans, or Pippins are suggested. Keep the apples overnight in a stone or enamel container (not metal). Cook the cores and peels in the kettle to remove the copper taste, then thoroughly clean the kettle with vinegar and salt.

The next morning before sunrise, put in enough water to cover the bottom of the kettle, add the apples, then begin cooking. Put in as many apples as can be stirred, situate the kettle over the fire but not touching the flames, and stir with the paddle. Bring to a boil and keep it bubbling. Add more apples as they cook down. *"Never cease stirring."*

In about six hours, gradually add the sugar—20 to 25 pounds for that quantity of apples, "depending on taste." Keep stirring another two to three hours. Just before removing the kettle from the fire, stir in 1/2 to 1 ounce of flavoring—oil of cinnamon or clove, sassafras, or vanilla. Put hot apple butter in jars and seal immediately. "Then go to sleep."

Mark & Betty Gatewood, Museum of American Frontier Culture, Staunton, VA. PHOTO ©WILLIAM B. FOLSOM

OPPOSITE: The valley of the James River. PHOTO ©TERRY DONNELLY

PAGE 36/37: Mabry Mill and pond. PHOTO ©MICHAEL COLLIER

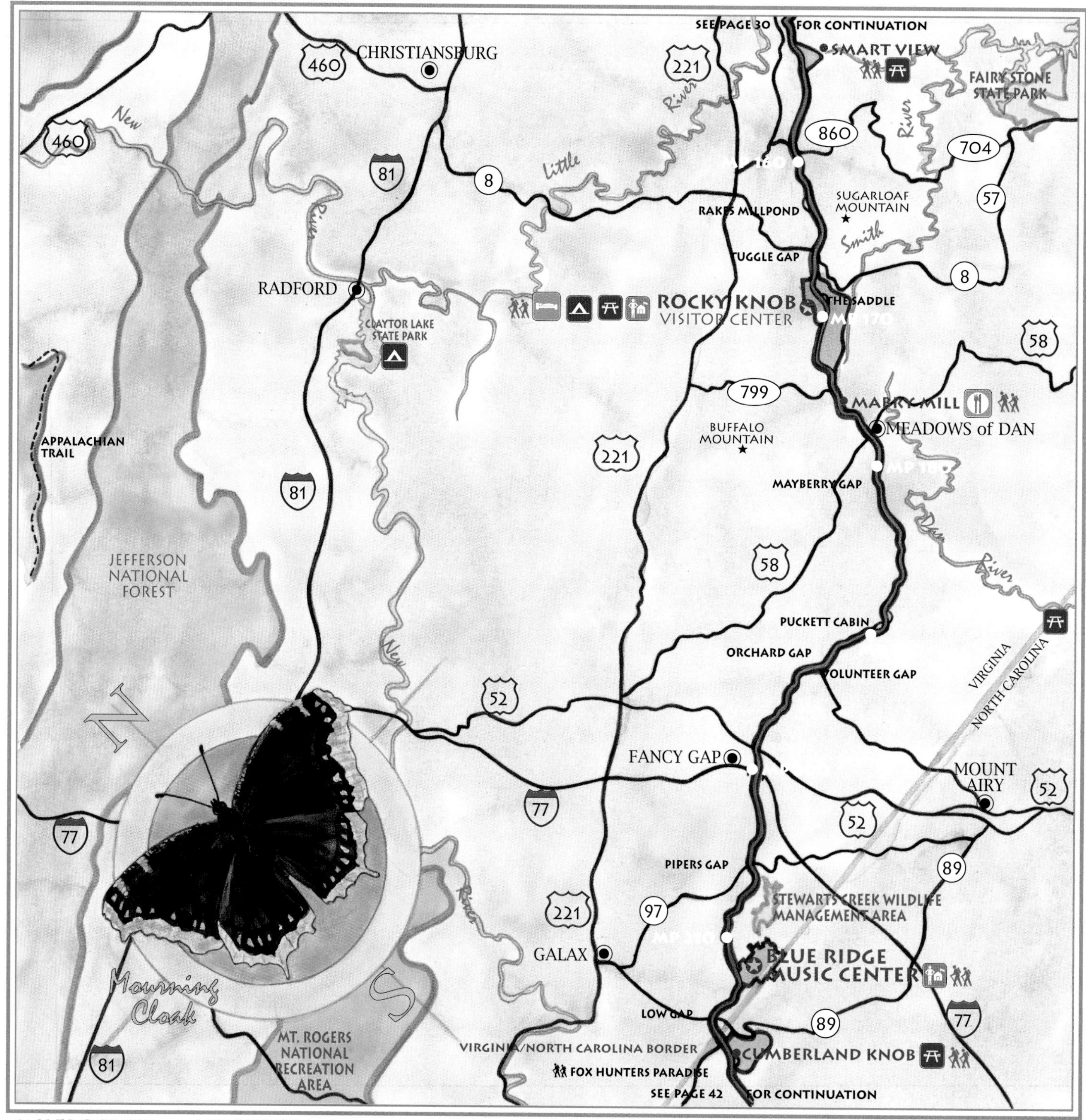

MILEPOST 150 TO **MILEPOST 220**

ILLUSTRATION BY DARLECE CLEVELAND

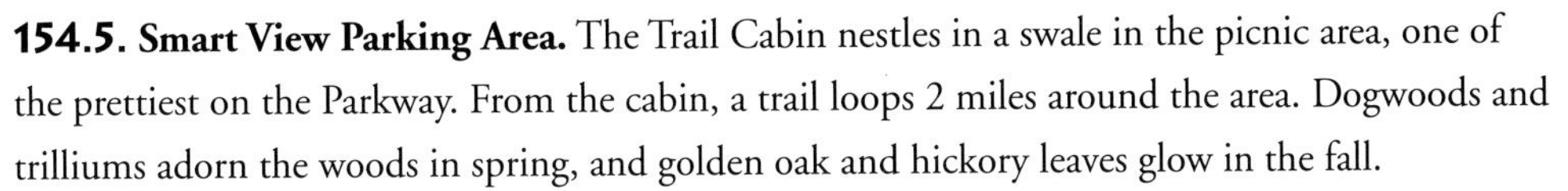

SMART VIEW TO CUMBERLAND KNOB

154.5. Smart View Parking Area. The Trail Cabin nestles in a swale in the picnic area, one of the prettiest on the Parkway. From the cabin, a trail loops 2 miles around the area. Dogwoods and trilliums adorn the woods in spring, and golden oak and hickory leaves glow in the fall.

165.3. Tuggle Gap. VA 8 Crossover. If you're anywhere near on a Friday night, head on down the state highway a few miles to the little town of Floyd for the Friday Night Jamboree at the country store, a great stop on the Virginia Heritage Music Trail.

167.0–174.0. Rocky Knob Recreation Area. This 4,500-acre area offers plentiful facilities including Rocky Knob Campground, a picnic area, visitor center, as well as the Rock Castle Gorge and Black Ridge trails. The demanding 10.8-mile Rock Castle Gorge Loop Trail descends 1,800 feet into the gorge, known for unusually rich plant life—some 25 species of ferns, 60 species of trees, and many different wildflowers. The remains of old homesites and mills speak of a once-thriving farming community. Rocky Knob Cabins, rustic housekeeping cabins at Mile 174, are available for rent.

176.1. Mabry Mill. A few miles south of the Rocky Knob area stands this elegant old gristmill with its overshot water wheel—an icon of the Blue Ridge Parkway. When water flows down the millrace, the giant wheel creaks as it turns, setting in motion a quartzite conglomerate grinding stone inside the mill. The scene has changed considerably since Ed Mabry was here. He built the mill around 1910; for more than two decades neighbors brought in a "turn" of corn—a bushel—to be ground into meal for their livestock and for their own cornbread, spoonbread, or grits. One-eighth of the meal was taken as a toll by the miller. The mill also powered a big saw. Mabry, a wheelwright and blacksmith, also repaired wagons. When Ed's health failed, his wife Lizzie took over the mill's operation.

Also on the grounds are a blacksmith shop, farm tools, one-room cabin, sorghum mill, and a bark mill, where oak and hemlock bark were ground and mixed with water to produce "bark liquor" used in tanneries. Another type of liquor was manufactured in the moonshine still, tucked away in the rhododendrons by the stream.

Mabry Mill is a lively place today—the miller gives talks, a blacksmith hammers glowing iron, while others make sorghum, apple butter, and ladderback chairs. A favorite tradition is the Sunday appearance of the Mabry Mill Band. Restaurant, gift shop, and restrooms are available.

177.7. US 58 Crossover, Meadows of Dan community.

180.1. VA 600, Mayberry Gap. A short detour off the Parkway is a trip back in time to the

TOP: Trail Cabin at Smart View.
PHOTO ©MICHAEL COLLIER
BOTTOM: Blooming trillium.
PHOTO ©LARRY ULRICH

TOP: Mayberry Trading Post. PHOTO ©MICHAEL COLLIER
MIDDLE: Buck rail fence at Groundhog Mountain. PHOTO ©MICHAEL COLLIER
BOTTOM: Snake rail fence at the Puckett Cabin. PHOTO ©JEFF GNASS

Mayberry Presbyterian Church and Mayberry Trading Post. The classic small country worship place is one of six rock churches built by the Reverend Bob Childress (others can be seen near the Rocky Knob cabins and at Bluemont, MP 191.9). Just down the road from the church is the Mayberry Trading Post, built in 1892. Coy Yeatts sits behind the counter, reading his Bible and tending the store, where a person can buy everything from fried pies and souvenir trinkets to rocks and homemade jelly. Look around, pull up a stool, and sit a spell. Mr. Yeatts, born and raised here, will happily discourse on any subject.

188.9. Groundhog Mountain. An interesting two-story observation tower stands on the hill here, with saddle-notched logs and a shed addition. Styled like a tobacco barn, the structure was used as a fire lookout. Sections of snake, buck, post-and-rail, and picket fences are displayed on the grounds. Each style had virtues, but nearly all were made of chestnut, prized for water- and rot-resistance and ease of working. A blight wiped out all the chestnut trees in the mountains in the 1930s. A large picnic area is also available for use.

189.9. Puckett Cabin. This small log cabin sits right by the Parkway, built by John Puckett for his brother's family, after his brother was killed in the Civil War. "Aunt" Betty Puckett lived here, next to her sister-in-law, Oreleana Puckett. "Aunt" Oreleana was famous in these parts as a midwife, a career that kept her busy toward the end of her long life. She died in 1939, at age 102.

199.4. Fancy Gap. US 52 Crossover.

212.5. Blue Ridge Music Interpretive Center. VA 612 Crossover. The outdoor stage and 3,000-seat amphitheater at the center have hosted mountain music concerts each Saturday in summer since 2001. The Interpretive Center, completed in July 2005, is open 7 days a week, from May to October, and includes a gallery, indoor auditorium, listening library, classroom, and music sales and information area. The National Council for the Traditional Arts operates the center, in cooperation with the National Park Service.

215.8. Low Gap. VA 89 Crossover leads to Galax, Virginia, and Mount Airy, North Carolina.

216.9. Virginia/North Carolina border. The Blue Ridge Mountains proved an insurmountable barrier to Colonel William Byrd as he attempted to survey the boundary between Virginia and North Carolina in 1728. Despite the difficulties, Byrd is credited as being one of the first to write about the mountains' distinctive blue haze: they "lookt like Ranges of Blue clouds rising one above another." The boundary survey was finally charted by Joshua Fry and Peter Jefferson (father of Thomas) in 1749.

217.5. Cumberland Knob. See page 43.

MUSIC OF THE BLUE RIDGE

Music is as much a part of the Blue Ridge as the mountains themselves. With little fanfare, somebody picks up a banjo, someone else grabs grandpa's fiddle, another a guitar, and you've got the makings of some good old-time "front porch" music. Anywhere, anytime, the foot-tapping tunes take hold and you just want to smile.

The area around Galax, Virginia, and Mount Airy, North Carolina, within a short distance of Cumberland Knob, is the heartland of traditional Blue Ridge music. The roots go deep here—in old ballads and hymns sung at home and in church, in road crew work songs, in folk, bluegrass, and string bands—entwined from cultural threads from Africa, Ireland, Scotland, and elsewhere.

You'll hear music at country stores, county fairs, campgrounds, and corn shuckings, in the honest refrains of "Uncle Pen," "Old Joe Clark," and "Go Tell Aunt Rhodie." And when things start warming up, cloggers and flatfooters do their fancy dances without inhibition. The region also boasts a large number of luthiers, makers of beautiful fiddles, banjos, dulcimers, and mandolins.

Since 2001, families, friends, and strangers have set up their lawn chairs and tapped their toes at the Blue Ridge Music Center's Saturday concerts. Now that the Blue Ridge Music Interpretive Center is open (it was completed in July 2005) more will be able to hear the good old-time songs wafting over the hills and hollows from the 3,000-seat outdoor amphitheater.

Old-time band performing at Mabry Mill. PHOTO ©PAT & CHUCK BLACKLEY

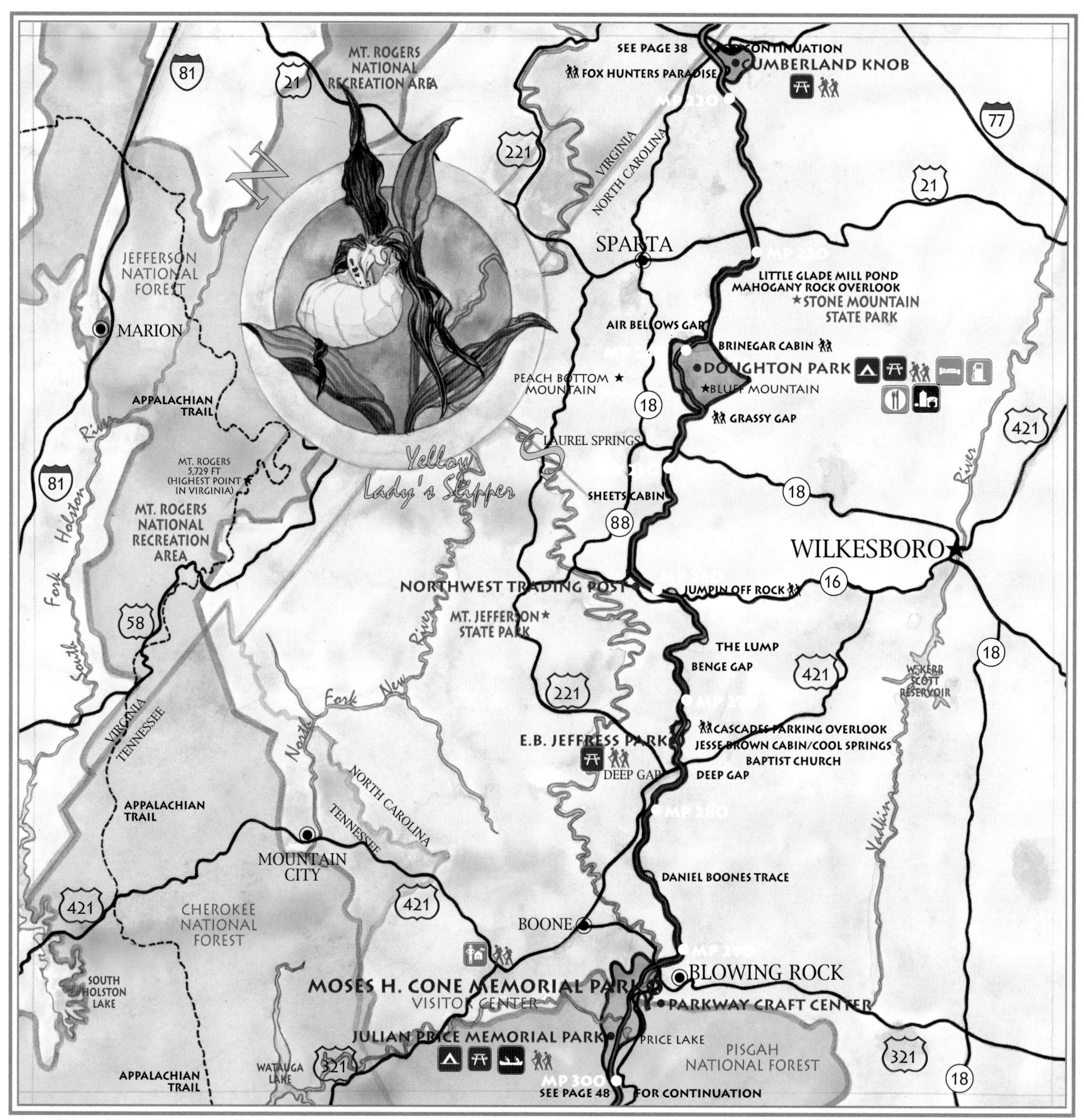

MILEPOST 215 TO MILEPOST 300

ILLUSTRATION BY DARLECE CLEVELAND

CUMBERLAND KNOB TO JULIAN PRICE MEMORIAL PARK

217.5. Cumberland Knob. The Blue Ridge Parkway leaves Virginia and enters North Carolina at Cumberland Knob. On a Monday morning in September 1935, more than a hundred men, eager to work, showed up here for the ground-breaking of the Parkway. They would build south for 12 1/2 miles through the coming year, completing the first section of the 469-mile road. Young Civilian Conservation Corps laborers built the wood-sided structure that was one used as a Visitor Center. There is a picnic area and two trails—a half-mile walk to the shelter on top of Cumberland Knob, and the longer 2-mile trail into Gulley Creek.

229.7. US 21 Crossover. East to Stone Mountain State Park, west to Sparta, NC

230.1. Little Glade Mill Pond. A good picnic stop with short walk around the lovely named Little Glade Mill Pond

235.0. Mahogany Rock Overlook. Another well-known location for hawk-watching in the fall. The gentler hills of Virginia roll away on one side, while on the other you'll see a hint of the ever-more rugged mountains of western North Carolina.

238.5. Brinegar Cabin. Martin and Caroline Brinegar built a modest two-room cabin here in 1877, with two stout stone chimneys, weatherboard siding, shake shingle roof, and south-facing porch. Caroline was a weaver, and inside the cabin is a four-poster loom. Martin died in 1925, but Caroline stayed on 10 more years, until the noise of the Parkway's construction drove her to leave her home and relocate in nearby Pine Swamp. The Brinegar barn, root cellar, and shaded springhouse—where cool water trickles sweetly—are still here too.

238.6-242.0. Doughton Park. This popular recreation area, once known as The Bluffs, was renamed for Congressman Robert Doughton, known to some as "Farmer Bob" and to others as the "father" of the Blue Ridge Parkway. The area features a campground, Bluffs Lodge, gas station, coffee shop, and access to 30 miles of trails on and around big, broad-backed Bluff Mountain. The Parkway runs alongside an impressive cliff known as Ice Rocks and the Alligator Back, and through rolling grassy meadows where white-tailed deer often congregate.

At the Wildcat Lookout at the lodge parking area, you can gaze down the steep mountainside to the one-room Caudill Cabin tucked into Basin Cove. Martin and Janie Caudill raised 14 children there in the late 1800s. One modern-day visitor wondered out loud "how fretful Miss Janie used to get" in such a small space with so many kids. In July 1916, a torrential flood and landslide swept away the whole community. Twelve people drowned, but the Caudill Cabin was unharmed. From Wildcat Rocks the Fodder Stack Trail is a 2-mile loop to Fodder

TOP: The Parkway near Doughton Park.
PHOTO ©PAT & CHUCK BLACKLEY
MIDDLE: The Brinegar Cabin.
PHOTO ©MICHAEL COLLIER
BOTTOM: Price Lake, early morning.
PHOTO ©JEFF D. NICHOLAS

PAGE 44/45: The Parkway as seen from near Low Gap. PHOTO ©LARRY ULRICH

TOP: Sheets Cabin. PHOTO ©MICHAEL COLLIER
BOTTOM: Jesse Brown Cabin (in distance) and Cool Springs Baptist Church. PHOTO ©PAT & CHUCK BLACKLEY

Stack Mountain and back.

243.7. Grassy Gap. Grassy Gap Fire Road can be followed for a 13-mile roundtrip hike or horseback ride; Basin Creek Trail, 6.5 miles roundtrip leaves from Grassy Gap Fire Road to the Caudill Cabin; Flat Rock Ridge Trail 10 miles to Basin Cove Creek and back.

248.1. NC 18 Crossover.

252.4. Sheets Cabin. Motorists get a glimpse of this simple one-room cabin, one of the oldest structures along the Parkway. Jess Sheets likely built it around 1815, and succeeding generations of the family lived here until 1940.

258.6. Northwest Trading Post. Wind chimes hang from the porch eaves, welcoming visitors to this shop stuffed with dulcimers, quilts, potholders, soap, dolls, baskets, brooms, bowls, and home-baked goods. White tags mark those made by residents of this part of northwest North Carolina.

261.0. NC 16 Crossover, Mount Jefferson State Park.

271.9. Cascades Parking Overlook/ E.B. Jeffress Park. The 0.6-mile trail to the cascades is sheer delight. In spring, flame azaleas blaze the path, along with the delicate white flowers of dog hobble and Solomon's seal. The trail goes down through the forest to Falls Creek. A log footbridge crosses the creek, and it's just a little farther down to the waterfall, plunging over a steep rocky stairstep. Falls Creek is bound for Yadkin Creek, the Pee Dee River, and finally the Atlantic Ocean in South Carolina. The trail leaves from the overlook; the park has picnic tables, restrooms, and drinking water. E.B. Jeffress was a state highway commissioner and strong Parkway booster.

272.5. Jesse Brown Cabin, Cool Springs Baptist Church. Jesse Brown built this basic log cabin sometime before 1840 about a half-mile from its present location. The Cool Springs Baptist Church was moved here too; it was really only a small wooden shelter where locals say circuit-riding preachers Bill Church and Willie Lee delivered the gospel. They stayed the night in the Brown cabin before continuing their rounds. Other research shows that the building was used as a barn.

276.4. Deep Gap. Hometown of Arthel "Doc" Watson.

285.1. Boone's Trace. Old Daniel himself may have crossed the Blue Ridge Mountains here, on his way to Kentucky. Another few miles down the road is an overlook of Yadkin Valley, where Boone made his home.

291.9. US 221/321 Crossover. To towns of Blowing Rock and Boone, NC

294.0. Moses H. Cone Memorial Park. Moses Cone built Flat Top Manor here as a summer place, and some summer home it was. Son of a German emigre, Cone and his brother Caesar worked in his father's grocery, but went on to prosper in the textile business. Moses became known as the "Denim King." Discovering the healthful atmosphere of the Blue Ridge Mountains, he and his wife Bertha built this estate on more than 3,500 acres, with the gracious porticoed house standing grandly on a hill overlooking their bucolic domain. He planted thousands of apple trees, and built lakes and 25 miles of carriage roads that now provide pleasant strolls. The Parkway Craft Center, open spring through fall, is located in the manor house, offering handicrafts. A National Park Service information desk and book sales area are also housed here.

297.1. Julian Price Memorial Park. Julian Price bought land here in the 1930s as a vacation spot for the employees of his company, Jefferson Standard Life Insurance Company. Price died in a car accident in 1946, and a few years later the company donated the land to the National Park Service for a recreation area. It includes picnic grounds, hiking trails, fishing, and the Parkway's largest campground with pleasant sites beside Price Lake. The lake was created by a dam on Boone Fork, a stream named for settler Jesse Boone, son (or nephew) of Daniel Boone. Boone Fork Trail, a 4.9-mile loop, leaves from the Price Park picnic area.

TOP: Early morning at Flat Top Manor, Moses H. Cone Memorial Park. PHOTO ©PAT & CHUCK BLACKLEY
BOTTOM: The view from near Cumberland Knob, autumn. PHOTO ©TIM FITZHARRIS

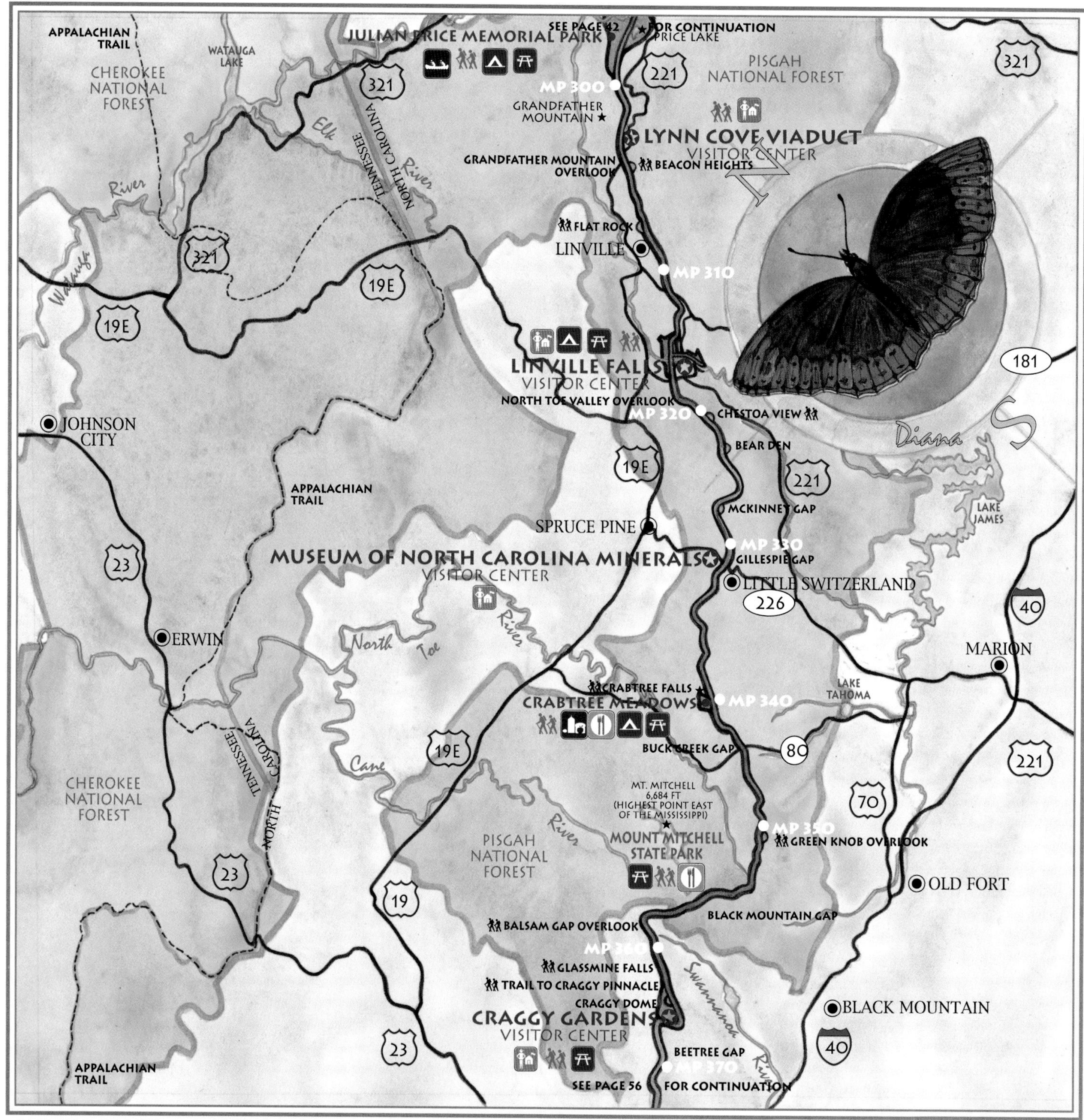

MILEPOST 295 TO **MILEPOST 370**

ILLUSTRATION BY DARLECE CLEVELAND

JULIAN PRICE MEMORIAL PARK TO CRAGGY GARDENS

297.1. Julian Price Memorial Park. See Page 47.

304.4. Linn Cove Viaduct. The Parkway's so-called "missing link," the Linn Cove Viaduct was part of the last 7 1/2 miles of the road to be built. An engineering wonder, the viaduct is a sweeping S-curved bridge skirting massive Grandfather Mountain. It required 153 pre-cast concrete sections, set by cranes onto seven piers, and extending for 1,243 feet. The viaduct was completed in 1983 and dedicated in 1987. The story of its construction is told in the visitor center here, and a short paved trail leads out for a closeup look at the underside of the viaduct.

This final segment was delayed while controversy swirled around protecting the special environment of Grandfather Mountain. The mountain, held by the Morton family, has been designated an International Biosphere Reserve in recognition of an unusually large number of globally imperiled plants and animals, such as spreading avens, Blue Ridge goldenrod, and the spruce-fir moss spider. At Grandfather Mountain, southbound Parkway travelers get a first glimpse of the high-elevation forest of red spruce and Fraser fir. Farther south into the Black Mountains, the road takes you into this forest.

305.2. Beacon Heights Parking Area. US 221 Crossover, exit for Grandfather Mountain and beginning of Tanawha Trail, 13.5 miles from Beacon Heights back to Julian Price Park. Tanawha is said to be the Cherokee name for Grandfather Mountain, and means hawk or eagle.

306.6. Grandfather Mountain Overlook. A framed view of the rugged quartzite mountain that rises to 5,964 feet, presiding over a good portion of this part of the Parkway

312.0. NC 181 Crossover.

316.4. Linville Falls Visitor Center. A helpful person in the visitor center orients people as they set out to see famed Linville Falls. A wall-sized map outside helps orient visitors too. There are two main trails—one to the Plunge Basin for a streamside view of the upper falls (1-mile roundtrip), and the second (1.6 miles roundtrip) leading to additional overlooks of the awesome lower falls that tumble 45 feet down into the narrow, dark Linville Gorge. Both paths lead past huge hemlocks and white pines and all three native rhododendrons: rosebay, Catawba, and Carolina.

317.4. US 221 Crossover.

318.4. North Toe Valley Overlook. View of North Toe River flowing from Tennessee into the Blue Ridge Mountain's rich mineral zone.

323.1. Bear Den Overlook. Another reference to the black bear. One reportedly holed up here

TOP: Grandfather Mountain seen from Flat Rock. PHOTO ©PAT & CHUCK BLACKLEY
BOTTOM: The bridge at Wilson Creek, Milepost 304. PHOTO ©MICHAEL COLLIER

TOP: Autumn from Green Knob. PHOTO ©MICHAEL COLLIER
BOTTOM: A brilliantly colored maple near Green Knob. PHOTO ©MICHAEL COLLIER

to evade hunters.

331.0. Gillespie Gap. NC 226 Crossover. Exit for Museum of North Carolina Minerals, with exhibits on the region's geology and gems and minerals. Mining in this region dates back at least 3,000 years when Native Americans excavated soapstone and mica. A gold rush here in the 1800s preceded the famous one in California. Mica, kaolin, and tungsten have all been dug, and today the nearby Spruce Pine District is the largest producer of feldspar in the world.

The Overmountain Victory Trail also crosses at this gap. In 1780, more than a thousand colonial troops passed through on their way to the victorious battle with the British at Kings Mountain in South Carolina. Museum also houses park visitor center and book sales area.

334.0. US 226A Crossover.

339.5. Crabtree Meadows. This major recreation area offers many delights for Parkway travelers: a quiet campground, picnic area, gift shop, and restaurant that boasts a local delicacy—pumpkin cobbler. The shop carries finely crafted baskets. Billy Bradshaw operated a corn mill on the creek here in the 19th century, when the area was known as Blue Ridge Meadows. A 2.5-mile loop trail leaves from the campground for Crabtree Falls, a 70-foot lacy veil of water. Save some energy for the steep ascent back out, and look for bloodroot, mayapple, Solomon's seal, and gentians blooming in various seasons.

344.0. Buck Creek Gap, NC 80 Crossover.

350.4. Green Knob Overlook. Lost Cove Ridge Trail (also known as Green Knob Trail) begins here. It's a half-mile to Green Knob itself, with a lookout tower. "Knob" is a term for a pointed mountain top.

355.4. Black Mountain Gap. Here NC 128 winds up 5 miles to Mount Mitchell State Park, North Carolina's oldest state park. The peak honors Dr. Elisha Mitchell, who began taking barometric measurements of mountains in the 1830s and 1840s. Contested by Thomas Clingman, Mitchell returned to remeasure some peaks; on the night of June 27, 1857, he slipped and fell down a waterfall and died. He is buried on top of the mountain that carries his name, and which at 6,684 feet above sea level is officially the highest point east of the Mississippi River.

359.0. Balsam Gap Overlook. Access to 6-mile Big Butt Trail and the Mountains-to-Sea Trail. Balsam is the local vernacular for red spruce and Fraser fir trees.

361.2. Glassmine Falls. Views of the wet-weather falls can be gained from the point and at the end of 0.1-mile trail. Mica, or isinglass, was mined nearby, hence the name.

364.2. Craggy Dome. A short trail (0.7 mile) climbs to Craggy Pinnacle, where rare plants—remnants from the Pleistocene—cling to the rocky summit. Hikers are asked to tread softly.

364.2-364.6. Craggy Gardens. See Page 57.

OPPOSITE: Spectacular Crabtree Falls. PHOTO ©LARRY ULRICH
PAGE 52/53: The Linn Cove Viaduct. PHOTO ©JERRY L. WHALEY

Catawba rhododendron. PHOTO ©TIM FITZHARRIS

AZALEAS AND RHODODENDRONS

Amid the white clouds and green forest, the lush purple-pink flowers of Catawba rhododendron flaunt their beauty. The blossom of this shiny-leaved shrub rightly deserves the accolade of signature flower of the Blue Ridge Parkway. In mid June at Craggy Gardens, hundreds of acres of them put on a stage-stopping floral show. Catawba rhododendron is a botanical specialty of the southern Appalachians, growing beneath the high-elevation spruce and fir trees and in tight tangles on heath balds, or "slicks" or "hells," as mountain people call them.

More common, and found at nearly all but the highest elevations, is the rosebay rhododendron. Pompons of white flowers cluster on the branches. This great rhododendron, as it is also commonly known, can reach tree size in favorable locations along shaded streams and on moist slopes. The less common Carolina rhododendron is found on a few rocky cliffs, notably in Linville Gorge.

The real Jezebel of the heath family is the flame azalea, wild honeysuckle in mountain parlance. When plant man William Bartram first saw the flame azalea around the time of the Revolutionary War, he declared it "certainly the most gay and brilliant flowering shrub yet known." Bartram applied the "fiery epithet" as the best description of the flowers, "which are in general of the color of the finest red lead, orange and bright gold, as well as yellow and cream...." Coming upon flame azaleas in bloom beside a trail, you'll catch your breath at the shocking sight of the flamboyant flowers. Hummingbirds and bees visit these flowers too, for the hidden riches of nectar. But that honey is said to be poisonous.

OPPOSITE: Azaleas and Lower Linville Falls in fog, Linville Gorge. PHOTO ©CARR CLIFTON

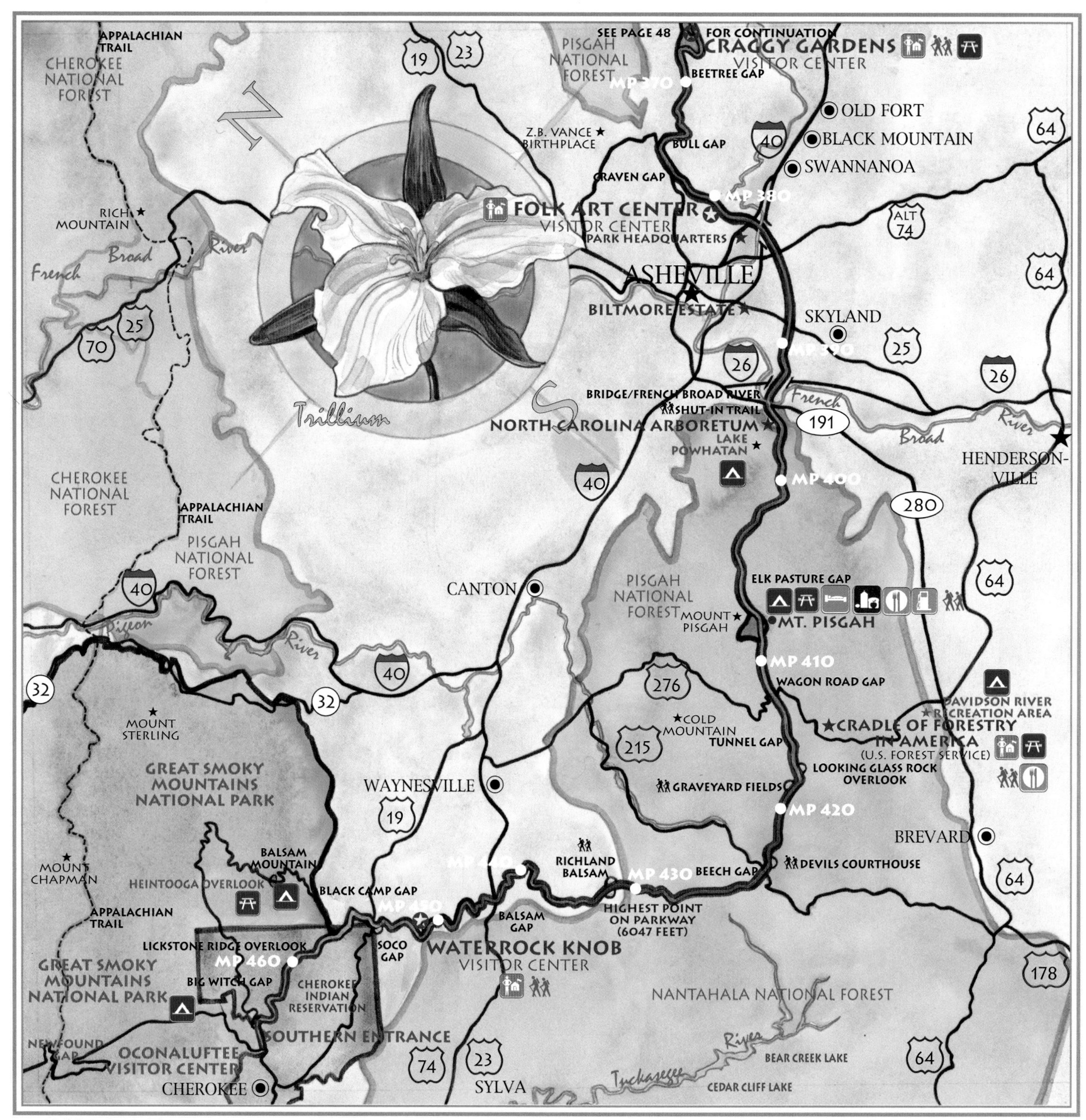

MILEPOST 365 TO **MILEPOST 469**

ILLUSTRATION BY DARLECE CLEVELAND

CRAGGY GARDENS TO SOUTH ENTRANCE

364.2-364.6. Craggy Gardens. The visitor center sits right beside the road, with helpful Park Service rangers on hand to answer questions. Most people want to know the exact timing of the spectacular rhododendron bloom. Catawba rhododendron, and the softer white rosebay rhododendron, reach their zenith around mid to late June, though some appear a bit earlier. From the visitor center, Craggy Gardens Trail (0.8 mile) leads to the large rustic shelter built by the CCC and on to the peaceful picnic area.

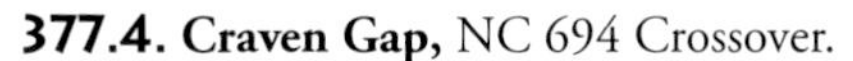

377.4. Craven Gap, NC 694 Crossover.

382.0. Folk Art Center, Southern Highland Craft Guild. The large windows and warm light of this graceful wood building invite visitors in to see some of the finest traditional and contemporary hand crafts being produced in the southern Appalachians today. Displayed in the galleries and sold in the Allanstand Craft Shop are quilts, pottery, basketry, brooms, weavings, toys, musical instruments, furniture, and jewelry—all unquestionably "hand-made objects of usefulness and beauty."

The center was opened in 1980, but its genesis dates to the early 20th century. An old bowknot design coverlet inspired Francis Goodrich to nurture the handcraft movement in the southern mountains. Her efforts, along with the early settlement schools and programs of the Russell Sage Foundation, led to the craft guild's founding in 1930 and realization of the dream of a center on the Blue Ridge Parkway 50 years later.

Park Service visitor information and sales area also housed in the center.

382.6. US 70 Crossover. Blue Ridge Parkway Headquarters—an administrative site, not a Visitor Center—is off the Parkway at 199 Hemphill Knob Road.

384.0. US 74A Crossover.

388.8. U.S. 25 Crossover. This road leads to Biltmore Estate, George Vanderbilt's famous 8,000-acre preserve and palatial 250-room French manor, high on a hill in south Asheville. Privately run. Admission fee for tours of home and gardens.

393.5. Bridge, French Broad River. Four major tributaries spill out of the mountains and meet to form the French Broad River. Here, just above Asheville, it's a wide, green, lazy river taking a northwesterly turn. When frontier hunters came through the Blue Ridge, they already knew of an English Broad River. Seeing this one flowing toward land then owned by France, they called it the French Broad in contrast. As the river's biographer Wilma Dykeman points out, to the Cherokee the river was Long Man, "whose head rested on the mountains, whose feet lay along the valleys,

TOP: Handcrafts on display, Folk Art Center. PHOTO ©BOB SCHATZ
BOTTOM: French Broad River. PHOTO ©BOB SCHATZ
BOTTOM: Maple leaf on folded gneiss, Graveyard Fields. PHOTO ©MICHAEL COLLIER

TOP: Crabtree Valley near Asheville, NC. PHOTO ©BOB SCHATZ
BOTTOM: Yellowstone Prong of the East Fork of the Pigeon River. PHOTO ©MICHAEL COLLIER
BOTTOM: Fog-shrouded forest near Richland Balsam Overlook. PHOTO ©JERRY L. WHALEY

who was fed by the Chattering Children of all his tributary streams."

393.6. NC 191 Crossover. North Carolina Arboretum, 426 acres of natural gardens, with learning center, nature walks, and other special events.

393.6. Shut-In Trail. George Vanderbilt used this trail to get from Biltmore Estate in Asheville to his Buck Spring hunting lodge in the Mount Pisgah area. Now a segment of the Mountains-to-Sea Trail, the Shut-In Trail runs for approximately 16 miles, with a nearly 3,000-foot elevation gain. It is accessible at this trailhead and at several other junctures along the Parkway to Mile 407.6.

405.5. Elk Pasture Gap, NC 151 Crossover.

407.0-410.0. Mount Pisgah Area. This is the last major developed area on the Parkway for southbound travelers. Here is a 137-site campground, picnic area, Pisgah Inn and restaurant, and access to several hiking trails along the Parkway and into Pisgah National Forest. Mount Pisgah itself rises to 5,721 feet; early settlers are said to have named it, believing they'd reached the promised land. You can find out for yourself by hiking up the 1.6-mile Mount Pisgah Trail to the summit. Other trails include Frying Pan and Buck Spring (to the site of Vanderbilt's hunting lodge). Spruce forests, red oak "orchards," and heath balds furnish botanical interest.

411.8. Wagon Road Gap, US 276 Crossover. Highway 276 leads 4 miles off the Parkway to the historic Cradle of Forestry in America site.

417.0. Looking Glass Rock Overlook. This is the platform from which to gaze upon the clear granite face of Looking Glass Rock, glistening when covered with water or ice. Also a fine place to watch the sun creep up over the mountains at dawn.

418.8. Graveyard Fields. A long time ago, winds blew down the fine old spruce trees and left a stump-littered landscape. The resulting mounds looked to someone like graves in a cemetery. Logging operations and the "Big Fire of 1925" ravaged the land again, and it is still recovering. A 2- to 3-mile loop trail crosses the Yellowstone Prong of the East Fork of the Pigeon River, and goes to Upper Yellowstone waterfall and Second Falls.

422.4. Devils Courthouse. This stark, sparsely vegetated mountain is said to be the place where the devil holds court in a cave. A steep 0.4-mile trail leads to the top and unending sights of mountain ridges, big river valleys, the Shining Rock Wilderness in Pisgah National Forest, and the states of South Carolina, Georgia, and Tennessee. Good hawk-watching perch.

423.2. Beech Gap, NC 215 Crossover.

431.4. Richland Balsam Overlook. At 6,047 feet, this is the highest point on the Parkway. Richland Balsam Mountain itself rises even higher, to 6,410 feet. A self-guiding trail to the top (about 1.4 miles) begins at the neighboring Haywood Jackson Overlook.

443.1. Balsam Gap, US 74 & 23 Crossover. In the southern Appalachians, the word "balsam" refers to the conifers that grace the highest elevations. Folk taxonomy includes both a "he-balsam," or red spruce, and a "she-balsam," the Fraser fir. The female version is distinguished by softer needles and white, resinous blisters on the bark.

451.2. Waterrock Knob. The small and inviting Park Service visitor center here has one wall of windows that looks out on the crest of the Great Smoky Mountains. A fire in the fireplace wards off the chill often present at these heights. A steep trail heads up Waterrock Knob, named for a spring that pours from under a rock. Many people take the walk as far as the first overlook at pavement's end, where they soak in the magnificent view of mountains in all directions—the Great Smokies to the west, the Cowees and Nantahalas to the southeast, and the Blacks and Craggies to the north. A few complete the half-mile to the summit—at 6,292 feet above sea level, the second highest peak on the Parkway. Waterrock Knob comes highly recommended for glorious sunsets.

455.7. Soco Gap, US 19 Crossover.

457.7. Cherokee Indian Reservation. The last 15 miles of the Blue Ridge Parkway pass through the land of the Eastern Band of the Cherokee, with tribal headquarters at the road's terminus in Cherokee, North Carolina.

458.2. Heintooga Ridge Road. Nine-mile spur road into Great Smoky Mountains National Park with overlooks, picnic area, and high, cool Balsam Mountain Campground (open in summer).

458.9. Lickstone Ridge Overlook. The word "lick" appears in several names along the Parkway, in reference to places where pioneers put out salt on a stone or in a log trough for their cattle. Good views of Cherokee land.

461.9. Big Witch Gap. View out toward the massive Great Smoky Mountains. An elder Cherokee man known as Big Witch, a gatherer of sacred eagle feathers and medicinal plants, lived in the valley. The nearby Big Witch Tunnel is the last of 26 along the Parkway. From here, the road descends another 2,000 feet to Great Smoky Mountains and its southern end.

469.0. Southern Terminus, Oconaluftee River Bridge. The end of the Blue Ridge Parkway is officially a tenth of a mile farther on, but for all practical purposes the Oconaluftee Bridge at Great Smoky Mountains National Park marks the conclusion. The broad Oconaluftee River and its rich floodplain valley was, and still is, home to the Cherokee. Oconaluftee, sometimes simply called "Luftee," derives from the name of the old Cherokee village, *E-gwan-ul-ti*, which means "by the river."

TOP: Looking Glass Rock.
PHOTO ©MICHAEL COLLIER
MIDDLE: Male northern cardinal.
PHOTO ©ADAM JONES
BOTTOM: Flame azalea.
PHOTO ©TERRY DONNELLY

PAGE 60/61: The Parkway near Waterrock Knob. PHOTO ©LARRY ULRICH

The Parkway near Milepost 454, autumn. PHOTO ©MICHAEL COLLIER

THE CRADLE OF FORESTRY IN AMERICA

The forests of the Blue Ridge are legendary, and so it is only fitting that this would be the Cradle of Forestry in America. The site's Forest Discovery Center, restored buildings, and two, well-groomed, paved trails—the Biltmore Campus Trail and Forest Festival Trail—commemorate the place where scientific forestry was born in the United States.

Inside the center, the film "Vanderbilt's Dream" tells the story. Seeking to remedy the devastating effects of overlogging in the mountains, George W. Vanderbilt bought 2,000 acres here in 1888. (He eventually owned 125,000 acres, land that is now Pisgah National Forest.) Vanderbilt hired the best men he could find to look at his land and come up with a healing prescription. Among them was Gifford Pinchot, soon to become the nation's first chief forester, and Pinchot's replacement, Carl Schenck.

In 1898, Schenck founded the Biltmore Forest School. The Biltmore Campus Trail leads past the reconstructed schoolhouse where he trained young men in then-revolutionary sustainable forestry practices. The science was so new that Schenck, trained in Germany, had to write the textbooks. Mornings were given over to classroom studies in botany, zoology, and silviculture, but in the afternoons Schenck and his students galloped away on horseback to see how the forest really worked. More than 300 young men were trained during the school's 15-year existence.

At age 86, Carl Schenck stated his abiding philosophy: "Woods are sanctuaries! Send the kids to the woods. They are better for them than any classrooms built of brick."

OPPOSITE: The blaze of autumn color along the Blue Ridge Parkway. PHOTO ©LAURENCE PARENT

THE NATURAL WORLD OF THE BLUE RIDGE MOUNTAINS

Driving the Blue Ridge Parkway in summer is like passing through a tunnel of green. Flanking both sides of the road, full-leaved trees cast shade and cloak the landscape in multiple layers and tones of emerald, lime, and olive.

This is the great Eastern Deciduous Forest of mixed hardwoods—oak, hickory, maple, walnut, black locust, yellow buckeye, tulip poplar, sourwood, and dogwood, to name only a few. In the richest, moistest mountain coves as many as forty different kinds of trees can be found. In fact, more than a hundred tree species have been identified in the park.

At first, it's difficult to pick out individuals, but observation of leaf shape, bark, nuts, and other traits will let you discern the various species: the deep indentations of maple leaves, the papery bark of birch, the pear-shaped nuts of hickories.

This forest obeys a beloved seasonal rhythm. In autumn, the greens change to orange, red, yellow, gold, and brown. The palette sweeps down the mountainsides in September, achieving dazzling beauty by mid to late October. The timing and intensity of the colors, many say, depends on the weather—warm, sunny days followed by cool nights. On fall weekends drivers jockey for position at Parkway overlooks, and you might think the blazing red of one maple could be drained away by all the pictures taken of it.

For the trees, this glowing spectacle is not put on for our benefit, but is the first step in preparation for the dry, cold conditions of winter. The pigments have been present in the leaves all along, masked by green chlorophyll. As the days shorten the chlorophyll disappears, photosynthesis shuts down, and the vibrant colors are revealed. The leaves finally flutter to the ground, contributing tons of biomass to replenish the soil. Without their leaves, each tree's unique architecture is beautifully displayed. Some green remains in the forest year-round, with the pines and graceful hemlocks.

From season to season, year-to-year, and century-to-century, the forest is constantly changing. Some trees die, leaving mounds of earth and windows for light where new seedlings can develop. This is all part of the normal life of a forest. Occasionally, though, larger-scale disturbances set back succession in a big way. The most momentous disturbance in the deciduous forest in recent times was the demise of the American chestnut, a species that once accounted for up to half of the forest canopy. In 1904 dying chestnuts were first noticed in New York. The cause was a fungus, *Endothia parasitica*, from Asia. The chestnut blight enters through a wound, attacks the tree's circulatory system, and kills the tree in short order. In a shockingly brief period, the blight

TOP: Fodder Stack Trail, Doughton Park.
PHOTO ©MICHAEL COLLIER
BOTTOM: Maidenhair fern.
PHOTO ©MICHAEL COLLIER

OPPOSITE: Rock Castle Gorge. PHOTO ©MICHAEL COLLIER

TOP: Tulip tree blossom. PHOTO ©CAROLYN FOX
MIDDLE: Mountain laurel near Rocky Knob. PHOTO ©MICHAEL COLLIER
BOTTOM: Lady's slipper near Smart View. PHOTO ©MICHAEL COLLIER

spread down the Appalachians. By 1930 nearly all the chestnut trees in North Carolina were infected. The loss of this premier species was tragic, not only for the forest and wildlife but also for mountain people. They relied on the fine wood of the chestnut, and obtained badly needed cash from selling the nuts.

Oaks and hickories moved in to fill the huge gap, but they've not fully assumed the important ecological role of chestnut. Stumps still stand here and there, and a few young sprouts grow bravely from them. But those seedlings do not manage to attain any age before the blight gets them. People haven't given up on the American chestnut, though, and researchers are working tirelessly toward its restoration. The main hope rests with backcrossing the native species with the Chinese chestnut, which is resistant to the blight, or possibly weakening the fungus. Their aim is to have American chestnut stock for replanting in a few years.

Around 5,000 feet in elevation, the mixed hardwood forest gives way to northern species such as beech and birch, along with curious "orchards" of red oak. They're called "orchards" here because the wind-pruned oaks resemble stunted apple trees. In past times, other cold-loving species grew in the mountains; a few still cling to pockets of coolness—like the small clump of large-toothed aspens along the Fodder Stack Trail at Doughton Park. The aspens are growing far enough south that Fraser magnolias, real southern belles, appear right beside them. On Mount Mitchell a few paper birch are found, also refugees from the last ice age.

Climbing another 500 feet or so in elevation, you enter a startlingly different forest. Fraser fir and red spruce adorn the cool, foggy heights. This is the boreal forest of Canada and the Far North, extending south along the highest backbone of the southern Appalachians. On the Parkway, the spruce-fir forest first appears at Milepost 306 in the vicinity of Grandfather Mountain. The trees' dark countenance and fresh scent also gave names to the Black Mountains and the Balsams. Although it does not cover much acreage, this forest type is hugely important for diversity—sheltering red squirrels, winter wrens, and rare specialists like the spruce-fir moss spider.

In the spruce-fir forest today, however, most of the Fraser firs are dead. Their ghostly skeletons are the work of a non-native insect, the balsam woolly adelgid. Spread on the wind and by animals, the adelgid moved south and began to infest firs on Mount Mitchell in the 1950s. Control efforts have been attempted, but are costly and only partly successful—they cannot keep up with the damage caused by the adelgids, which have killed nearly all the Fraser firs in the southern Appalachians. There is hope in the survival of some older fir specimens, but for one of the two dominant trees of the unique spruce-fir forest of the southern mountains, it is too late.

Notable for an absence of trees are places called balds, open areas of grasses and heath plants in the mountains. Craggy Gardens is the most famous on the Parkway, a mix of both grass and heath. The origin of balds is much debated among ecologists. Fire and grazing are the main explanations, though the jury is still out. Whatever the cause, hawthorn and other shrubs and trees are encroaching on grassy balds. In the Blue Ridge, a few representative samples are maintained by mowing or burning.

In spring, the monotone of winter is broken with the joyous sight of the first wildflowers—bloodroot, violets, and irises poking up through the duff, followed by solitary lady slipper orchids, explosions of trilliums, dainty mayapple flowers, and the curious Jack-in-the-pulpit, hardly a flower at all. From March, April, and into early May, before the trees fully leaf out, the bloom is riotous. As the canopy closes overhead, only goldenrod, fire pink, Joe-pye weed, and a few others extend themselves to reach the sun.

Wildflowers captured the hearts of two local women, Helen Smith and her sister Julia. They spent their lives photographing and cataloging the flora of the Blue Ridge Parkway, and persuaded crews to reduce mowing along the roadsides to let the flowers bloom.

While the flowers are tried and true crowd pleasers, another part of the botanical world exists beneath the trees. It includes glossy-leaved galax, long gathered by mountain people and sold during the winter holidays; tall ferns; cushiony mosses; and literally thousands of species of mushrooms and fungi in all shapes, sizes, and colors.

In any environment plants sustain animals, from the smallest insect to the biggest, cuddly mammal. As far as cuddly mammals go, the one that could easily be adopted as mascot of the Blue Ridge Parkway is the groundhog. This chunky brown rodent, also called a woodchuck, is a loner; it's commonly seen along the roadside, but never strays too far from deeper cover. Groundhogs also inhabit

TOP: Passion flower growing on barb-wire fence. PHOTO ©ADAM JONES
MIDDLE: Turk cap lilies. PHOTO ©PAT & CHUCK BLACKLEY
BOTTOM: Fire pink near Rocky Knob. PHOTO ©MICHAEL COLLIER

PAGE 68/69: Dogwood and azaleas near Otter Creek. PHOTO ©LARRY ULRICH

TOP: Groundhog (or woodchuck). PHOTO ©ADAM JONES
MIDDLE: White-tailed deer.
PHOTO ©MICHAEL J. HICKEY/PLACEPHOTO.COM
BOTTOM: Black bear. PHOTO ©CHUCK SUMMERS

grassy balds, along with meadow voles and meadow jumping mice. Gray squirrels are ever-present, scampering along tree trunks, building nests of leaves, and voraciously eating or storing acorns and hickory nuts to carry them through the winter. In fact, the gray squirrel's fate from year to year is closely tied to acorn abundance.

Raccoons, opossums, and skunks—what one naturalist calls the "opportunists of the mountains"—eat nearly anything and are well adapted to human company. Common though these smaller mammals are, it is the charismatic big mammals—especially deer and bear—that are the real traffic stoppers. In early morning and evening, white-tailed deer graze along the Parkway and nibble tender shoots and twigs. These adaptable herbivores are animals of the edge between forest and field, where they stand ever alert to bound away into the woods. Their main predators—wolves and mountain lions—are mostly gone from the mountains today, but bobcats are still around to prey on the whitetails. (American elk and woodland bison were extinguished in this part of the country by the early 1800s.)

Black bears are not common, but their numbers are increasing and they are seen occasionally. In the neighboring Great Smokies and Shenandoah National Parks, bears reach some of their greatest densities in the East. Parkway place names—Bear Pen, Bearwallow, Bear Trail—tell of this animal's history here, as do the long legends of the hunters, men like "Bar" Tolley, who followed his hounds through the tortuous laurel tangles in pursuit of his prey.

With upwards of 60 inches of rain fairly evenly distributed through the year, the Blue Ridge Mountains abound with streams and wetlands. Marshes, swamps, and bogs intersperse the forests, harboring frogs, toads, and turtles. The rare bog turtle reaches its farthest southern limits on the Parkway, and its habitat has been declared "globally rare." Beavers, reintroduced to the mountains, are helping maintain the bogs. Small vernal pools, those that fill mostly in early spring, exist long enough each year for wood frogs, spring peepers, and some salamanders to lay eggs in them. In fact, the southern Appalachians serve as a repository of an unparalleled salamander diversity. More than 30 species have been tallied in the park—among them the spotted, marbled, dusky, pigmy, three-lined, four-toed, not to mention the Peaks of Otter salamander that is found nowhere else in the world.

The mountains are equally rich in birdlife. The sharp scrawks of blue jays and the cawing of crows fill the deep woods. Cousins, these two are the most readily seen—and heard—resident birds, along with others such as dark-eyed juncos, pileated woodpeckers, and cardinals. The park's great elevation range and multiple habitats mean birders can find red-breasted nuthatches and golden-crowned kinglets in the spruce-fir forest, great blue herons beside ponds, eastern meadowlarks in fields, and gaggles of wild turkeys on the shoulder of the road.

The long north-south axis of the Blue Ridge also serves as a natural corridor for migrating birds in spring and fall. In autumn, especially, millions of birds sweep down from the north, feeding on the bright red berries of spicebush, dogwood, and sumac. Tanagers, grosbeaks, warblers, vireos, and other songbirds are among the dozens of species known as "neotropical migrants," ones that spend winters in Central and South America and return north in spring to breed. Another great avian movement begins in mid September and lasts until early November. On a good day in October perhaps a thousand broad-winged hawks will swirl up out of the bluish valley haze, catch thermals, and rocket down the ridgelines on epic journeys south. Joining them are kestrels, ospreys, harriers, merlins, and the occasional peregrine falcon or eagle.

While hawk watchers are counting raptors in the fall, they can't miss another airborne migrant—not a bird but a butterfly. As days shorten and nights grow colder each autumn, monarch butterflies stop mating and reproducing, and instead spend their energy imbibing nectar from flowers, fueling themselves for a long journey. They migrate down the spine of the Appalachians, as birds do, fluttering by like leaves. Some monarchs will stop short in Texas or other Gulf states, while others continue to Mexico to a prime overwintering site in the Sierra Madre. In March, the butterflies head back north, courting and mating along the way. That generation dies midway, however, and the newborns finish the 2,000- to 3,000-mile roundtrip. These orange and black beauties are really "milkweed on the wing"—through their entire life cycle monarchs rely almost exclusively on milkweed. They take up toxic compounds from the plants, and any predator that sinks into one will be greeted with a distinct distastefulness.

Whatever your interests, the more than 92,000 acres of the Blue Ridge Parkway are a naturalist's dream world, with something exciting happening every day.

TOP: Blue jay. PHOTO ©ADAM JONES
MIDDLE: Male scarlet tanager. PHOTO ©ADAM JONES
BOTTOM: Tiger swallowtail butterfly.
PHOTO ©WILLIAM B. FOLSOM

Balsam firs, killed by the balsam woolly adelgid, atop Mt. Mitchell, Mount Mitchell State Park. PHOTO ©TOM TILL

THREATS TO THE PARKWAY

The Blue Ridge Parkway faces a frightening prospect with the appearance of another non-native insect, this time the hemlock woolly adelgid. Eastern hemlocks in Shenandoah National Park have already been devastated, and trees in both the Smoky Mountains and along the Parkway now are threatened as well. This adelgid acts as swiftly and is as deadly as the balsam woolly adelgid. Both the beautiful old eastern hemlocks, and the rarer Carolina hemlocks, may be infected and killed in only a few years. No one can yet predict what the loss of these trees will mean; but without their generous shading of streams, all kinds of animals from brook trout to ruffed grouse could be affected. A predatory beetle has been released, but it's still to early to tell whether it can make a dent in the adelgid invasion. Exotic plants including kudzu, Oriental bittersweet, lespedeza, and mustards have also made incursions along the Parkway.

In streams, introduced rainbow and brown trout have outcompeted native brook trout, and fisheries biologists are trying to remove the non-natives to save the brookies. Amphibians—whose population declines have been partly attributed to environmental problems—are being closely watched. On the Parkway, steps are being taken to restore valuable wetlands by fencing out cattle, and beavers are aiding in the task. Non-native birds are a menace as well. Starlings displaced eastern bluebirds, but nest boxes installed along the Parkway are encouraging bluebirds to reestablish homes.

Biologists are studying one bird—the cerulean warbler—that summers among the tallest trees of mature open hardwoods. This warbler is a neotropical migrant whose numbers declined precipitously in the 1990s, likely due to loss of forests in the tropics and in the United States.

Such fragmentation of habitat is the biggest threat in the Blue Ridge Mountains. Housing, industries, and roads are all impinging on the Parkway's stupendous scenery and wildlife habitat. Long and narrow in shape, with nearly 1,200 miles of boundary, the park feels development right up to the edge in many places. The lesson, as one observer put it, is that you "don't eat your seed corn." And with the lack of land-use planning and sustainable practices, "right now we're eating our seed corn right and left."

Recognizing imminent and possibly irrevocable harm, in 2003 the nonprofit group Scenic America designated a 28-mile stretch of the Parkway through the Roanoke, Virginia, area as a "last chance landscape." The hope is that government officials and private landowners will cooperate to protect the heroic Blue Ridge views.

OPPOSITE: Oaks and ridges seen from near Humpback Mountain. PHOTO ©CARR CLIFTON

TRAIL OF TEARS: THE CHEROKEE

Near present-day Cherokee, North Carolina, at the southern end of the Blue Ridge Parkway, stands an earthen mound known as *Kituhwa*. The Cherokee say this is their place of origin. They have lived in this region for a long time—when Spanish conquistador Hernando de Soto passed through in 1540; when Revolutionary soldiers fought battles here; and when the first white settlers spilled through the mountain gaps to builds homes and farm the river bottoms.

The Cherokee themselves were village-dwelling farmers. They traded widely, developed an alphabet and a newspaper, and had their own constitution. But by the early 1800s the flood of newcomers washing across the mountains saw their land and coveted it. In 1829, gold was discovered in north Georgia. By that time, the Cherokee and other eastern Indians were viewed only as an obstacle to be removed.

Treaty after treaty was signed with the United States government, ceding Indian lands. The states also passed laws attempting to deprive Indians of their land and minerals. In the federal Removal Act, Congress gave President Andrew Jackson the authority to negotiate with the Indians to exchange their lands in the East for land in Indian Territory west of the Mississippi River.

The Cherokee had already seen their neighbors, the Choctaw and Chickasaw, outwitted, subdued, and removed from their homelands. In 1835, they signed the New Echota Treaty, giving up all their land east of the Mississippi for $5 million from the government and land in the west. Three years later, General Winfield Scott and his troops began rounding up the Cherokee, holding them in internment centers, then ushering them to Oklahoma. Some of the people went by boat on rivers, while most went overland, in wagons or on foot, in the fall of 1838. It took nearly a year—15,000 Cherokee eventually were removed, and 4,000, perhaps as many as 8,000, died of disease, malnourishment, or exposure. The $5 million was never paid.

Leader Tsali and a small group of Cherokee escaped and hid deep in the Smoky Mountains. Pursued by the military, Tsali finally surrendered to save his family and was executed. The Cherokee who were left formed the Eastern Band, and lands they repurchased became the Qualla Reservation. Enrolled members now number more than 11,000.

To this day, the Cherokee tell the legend of a plant called the corn bead. It began to grow where the people wept as the soldiers drove them west on the Trail of Tears. Wherever they fall, seeds of the corn bead take root and grow into strong, stubborn plants.

Cherokee Chief Sequoyah, creator of the Cherokee alphabet. ILLUSTRATION COURTESY LIBRARY OF CONGRESS

OPPOSITE: Sunset over the Great Smoky Mountains as seen from the southern Blue Ridge Parkway. PHOTO ©CARR CLIFTON

PAGE 76/77: The Parkway, early spring. PHOTO ©TERRY DONNELLY

BLUE RIDGE PARKWAY FACILITIES

BLUE RIDGE PARKWAY FACILITIES & VISITOR SERVICES

Milepost	Location	Visitor Center	Book or Craft Sales	Demonstrations	Gasoline	Food	Lodging	Picnicking	Self-Guiding Trails	Ranger Talks	Camping	Camp Store	Hiking	Fishing	Canoe/Boat Rentals
VIRGINIA															
5.8	HUMPBACK ROCKS	●	●	●				●	●	●			●		
60.9	OTTER CREEK		●			●				●	●		●	●	
63.8	JAMES RIVER	●	●					●	●				●	●	
86.0	PEAKS OF OTTER	●	●	●	●	●	●	●	●	●	●	●	●	●	
120.4	ROANOKE MOUNTAIN									●	●		●		
154.5	SMART VIEW							●					●		
169.0	ROCKY KNOB	●	●				●	●	●	●	●		●		
176.1	MABRY MILL		●	●		●			●						
NORTH CAROLINA															
212.5	BLUE RIDGE MUSIC CENTER	●	●	●					●						
217.5	CUMBERLAND KNOB							●					●		
238.5	BRINEGAR CABIN			●									●		
241.1	DOUGHTON PARK		●		●	●	●	●		●	●	●	●	●	
258.6	NORTHWEST TRADING POST		●	●											
272.0	E. B. JEFFRESS PARK							●	●				●		
294.1	MOSES H. CONE MEM. PARK	●	●	●					●	●			●	●	
297.1	JULIAN PRICE MEM. PARK							●		●	●		●	●	●
304.4	LINN COVE VIADUCT	●	●										●		
316.4	LINVILLE FALLS	●	●					●		●	●		●	●	
331.0	MUSEUM OF N.C. MINERALS	●	●	●											
339.5	CRABTREE MEADOWS		●			●		●		●		●	●		
364.6	CRAGGY GARDENS	●	●					●	●		●		●		
382.0	FOLK ART CENTER	●	●	●						●					
408.6	MOUNT PISGAH		●		●	●	●	●	●	●	●	●	●		
451.2	WATERROCK KNOB	●	●										●		

EMERGENCY & MEDICAL

24-HOUR SERVICE—Dial 911
Emergencies & Accidents: 800-727-5928

ROAD CONDITIONS

828-298-0398

FOR MORE INFORMATION

Blue Ridge Parkway Headquarters
199 Hemphill Knob Road
Asheville, NC 28803
(828) 271-4779
www.nps.gov/blri

Blue Ridge Parkway Association
P.O. Box 2136
Asheville, NC 28802
www.blueridgeparkway.org

Eastern National
210 Riceville Road
Asheville, NC 28805
(828) 298-2774
www.easternnational.org

Blue Ridge Foundation
P.O. Box 10427, Salem Station
Winston-Salem, NC 27108
(336) 721-0260
www.brpfoundation.org

Friends of the Blue Ridge Parkway
P.O. Box 20986
Roanoke, VA 24018
800-228-7275
www.blueridgefriends.org

LODGING INSIDE THE PARK

Rocky Knob Cabins
540-593-3503
(Memorial Day through early fall)
540-952-2947 (off-season)

Peaks of Otter Lodge (open year-round)
540-586-1081

Bluffs Lodge/Doughton Park
336-372-4499

Pisgah Inn
828-235-8228

CAMPING INSIDE THE PARK

Most campgrounds are first-come, first-serve*
Otter Creek (MP 60.8)
Peaks of Otter (MP 86)
Roanoke Mountain (MP 120.4)

Rocky Knob (MP 167)
Doughton Park (MP 241.1)
Price Park* (MP 297.1)
Linville Falls* (MP 316.4)
Crabtree Meadows (MP 339.5)
Mount Pisgah (MP 408)

***NOTE:** Advance reservations may be made online for portions of the campgrounds at Linville Falls and Price Park at **www.reserveUSA.com** or by phoning 1-877-444-6777.

LODGING OUTSIDE THE PARK

Waynesboro Office of Tourism
301 W. Main Street,
Waynesboro, VA 22980
866-253-1957 (toll-free)

Lynchburg Visitor Center
12th and Church Streets
Lynchburg, VA
800-732-5821

Roanoke Convention and Visitors Bureau
114 Market Street
Roanoke, VAS 24011
800-635-5535

Boone Convention and Visitors Bureau
208 W. Howard Street
Boone, NC 28607
800-852-9506

Blowing Rock Chamber of Commerce
P.O. Box 406
Blowing Rock, NC 28605
828-295-7851

Asheville Convention and Visitors Bureau
P.O. Box 1010
Asheville, NC 28802
800-280-0005

CAMPING OUTSIDE THE PARK

George Washington National Forest
5162 Valleypointe Parkway
Roanoke, VA 24019
888-265-0019

Pisgah National Forest
160A Zillicoa Street
Asheville, NC 28802
828-257-4200

Mount Mitchell State Park
2388 Highway 128
Burnsville, NC 28714
828-675-4611
Nine sites, tents only

OTHER REGIONAL SITES

Appalachian Trail
Appalachian Trail Conference
P.O. Box 807
Harpers Ferry, WV 25425
304-535-6331

Biltmore Estate
1 Approach Road
Asheville, NC 28803
800-624-1575

Cherokee Indian Reservation
P.O. Box 460
Cherokee, NC 28719
800-438-1601
The story of the Trail of Tears is enacted each summer in the outdoor drama, "Unto These Hills," in the town of Cherokee. Other attractions include Museum of the Cherokee Indian, Qualla Arts and Crafts Mutual, and the Oconaluftee Indian Village.

Cradle of Forestry in America
1001 Pisgah Highway
U.S. Highway 276
Pisgah Forest, NC 28768
828-877-3130

Grandfather Mountain
2050 Blowing Rock Highway
Linville, NC 28646
800-468-7325

Great Smoky Mountains National Park
107 Park Headquarters Road
Gatlinburg, TN 37738
865-436-1200
www.nps.gov/grsm

North Carolina Arboretum
100 Frederick Law Olmsted Way
Asheville, NC 28806
828-665-2492

Shenandoah National Park
3655 US Highway 211E
Luray, VA 22835
540-999-3500
www.nps.gov/shen

Virginia's Explore Park
Milepost 115, Blue Ridge Parkway
PO Box 8508
Roanoke, VA 24014
800-842-9163

The **BLUE RIDGE PARKWAY DIRECTORY AND TRAVEL PLANNER** is published by the Blue Ridge Parkway Association and is distributed free at all Parkway visitor centers. It is the most complete and up-to-date guide available to attractions, outdoor recreation, accommodations, restaurants, shops, and a variety of other services essential to travelers.

SUGGESTED READING

Bake, William A. *Mountains and Meadowlands Along the Blue Ridge Parkway.* National Park Service: Washington, D.C. 1975.

Catlin, David T. *A Naturalist's Blue Ridge Parkway.* University of Tennessee Press: Knoxville, TN 1984, 1992.

Johnson, Randy. *Hiking the Blue Ridge Parkway.* Falcon/Globe Pequot Press: Guilford, CT. 2003.

Jolley, Harley. *The Blue Ridge Parkway.* University of Tennessee Press: Knoxville, TN. 1969.

Logue, Victoria, Frank Logue, and Nicole Blouin. *Guide to the Blue Ridge Parkway.* Eastern National: Ft. Washington, PA. 2003.

Lord, William. *Blue Ridge Parkway Guide.* Vols. 1 and 2, Menasha Ridge Press: Birmingham, AL. 1992.

Mitchell, Anne Virginia. *Parkway Politics: Class, Culture, and Tourism in the Blue Ridge.* Doctoral Dissertation, University of North Carolina: Chapel Hill, NC. 1997.

Nash, Steve. *Blue Ridge 2020.* University of North Carolina Press: Chapel Hill, NC. 1999.

Olson, Ted. *Blue Ridge Folklife.* University Press of Mississippi: Jackson, MS. 1998.

Rives, Margaret Rose. *Blue Ridge Parkway: The Story Behind the Scenery.* KC Publications: Las Vegas, NV. 1997.

PRODUCTION CREDITS

Publisher: Jeff D. Nicholas
Author: Rose Houk
Editor: Nicky Leach
Illustrations: Darlece Cleveland
Printing Coordination: Tien Wah Press

ISBN 1-58071-061-1
ISBN 13: 9781-58071-061-9

Printed in the Republic of South Korea.
First printing, Spring 2006.

SIERRA PRESS
4988 Gold Leaf Drive
Mariposa, CA 95338
e-mail: siepress@sti.net

www.NationalParksUSA.com

OPPOSITE
Roan Mountain. PHOTO ©LAURENCE PARENT
BELOW
Red maples along the Parkway.
PHOTO ©LARRY ULRICH